BACKROADS

of

MICHIGAN

BACKROADS

— of —

MICHIGAN

*Your Guide to Michigan's Most
Scenic Backroad Adventures*

TEXT AND PHOTOGRAPHY BY
ROBERT W. DOMM

Voyageur Press

DEDICATION

To donna

MBI Publishing Company titles are also available at discounts in bulk quantity for industrial or sales-promotional use. For details write to Special Sales Manager at MBI Publishing Company, Galtier Plaza, Suite 200, 380 Jackson Street, St. Paul, MN 55101-3885 USA

ISBN-13: 978-0-7603-2574-2
ISBN-10: 0-7603-2574-X

Editor: Jeni Henrickson
Designer: Maria Friedrich

Printed in China

ON THE COVER:
A classic Michigan backroad.

ON THE TITLE PAGES:
Pictured Rocks National Lakeshore on Lake Superior became the nation's first national lakeshore in 1966.

INSET ON THE TITLE PAGES:
Michigan's 3,251 miles of Great Lakes shoreline are dotted with dozens of unique and interesting lighthouses.

CONTENTS

INTRODUCTION

FACING PAGE:
The crescent moon hangs low in the morning sky over Kingston Lake in the Pictured Rocks National Lakeshore.

ABOVE:
Michigan contains thousands of lakes, from shallow ponds to several of the largest freshwater lakes in the world.

I must confess that I had forgotten a lot about Michigan, the state in which I have spent my entire life. Not only had many of the colorful aspects of my state's history faded from my memory, but I had also forgotten how exploring the landscape of Michigan can leave you grateful for living in such an extraordinary place. At one time or another, I have visited nearly every corner of both peninsulas—as a vacationer, a fisherman, a canoeist, a backpacker, a photographer, or as a visitor to friends and family. Many of the byways I chose to include in this book I last visited many years ago, and the intimate details of these places had faded from my memory. In this light, *Backroads of Michigan* has been a journey of discovery for me, just as I hope it will be for you.

As I revisited these backroads in search of fresh photographs, I stopped to talk to the people who live along the routes, and it struck me that the story of Michigan's backroads goes beyond postcard photography and checklists of places to visit. Every route described in this book is a route through the lives of people, living and dead; through forests and landscapes of the present and past; and through an environment of constant change and sublime beauty.

To approach this book as merely a tour guide to Michigan at the turn of the twenty-first century would be a disservice to the people and the history that make our state the incredible place it is. It would render only a superficial understanding of why the people of Michigan treasure their state and why they choose to live, work, and even vacation here. Each of the twenty-five backroad journeys found in this book follows modern byways, but each route also travels the backroads of history and legend.

An abundance of publicly held land guarantees Michigan's citizens and visitors access to the state's abundant natural wonders. Hiking, skiing, horseback riding, snowmobiling, mountain biking, and backpacking trails crisscross Michigan's forests and parks. While there is plenty to see through the windshield, make sure you pack hiking boots or cross-country skis as the season dictates: you don't want to miss the chance to see Michigan's wild country up close and personal.

Along with its magnificent forests and backcountry, Michigan also boasts an awesome array of waterways. From the retreat of the Wisconsin Glacier, ten thousand years ago, to the present time, water has defined human activity in Michigan. It carried the birchbark and dugout canoes of Michigan's Ottawa, Chippewa, and Potawatomi peoples. When the French traders and Jesuit missionaries arrived, water routes led them to new converts, new markets for their goods, and on voyages of discovery into North America's interior. During the nineteenth century, the Great Lakes and their tributaries floated Michigan timber, copper, and iron ore to market, and

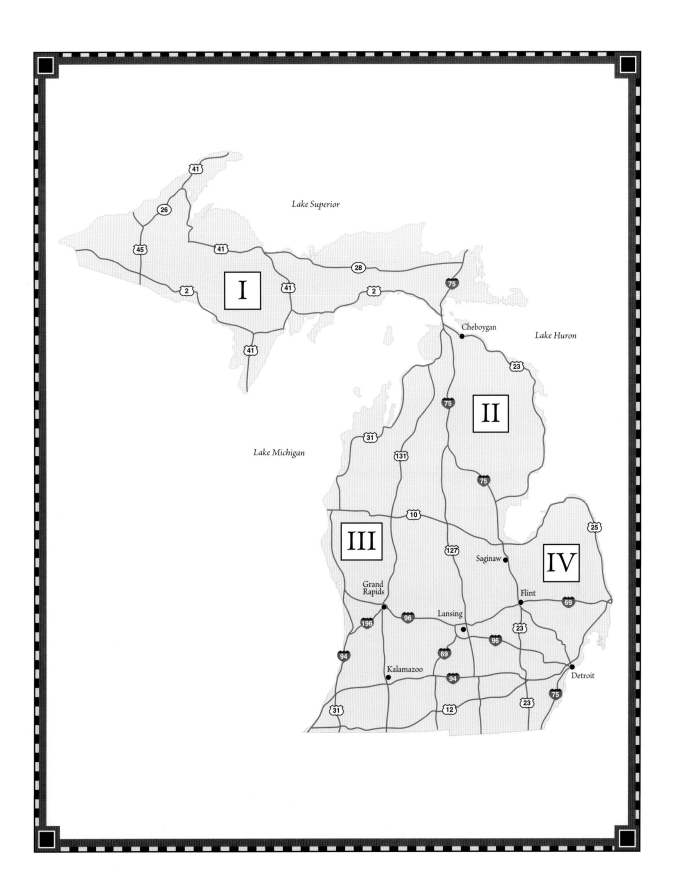

The farm country of Southern Michigan produces a variety of crops including corn, soybeans, potatoes, and grains.

The call of the sandhill crane can be heard from wetlands all over Michigan. Once rare in the state, the cranes have made a stunning comeback, particularly in Southern Michigan and the eastern Upper Peninsula.

Sundew is one of the many interesting plants found in Michigan's bogs. The sticky fluid on the tips of its leaf hairs entraps insects which are then digested by the small carnivorous plant.

Monarch butterflies feed on goldenrod nectar before starting their generational migration south.

A young gray tree frog rests on a fern frond. Michigan is home to fourteen species of frogs and toads.

In the days before the steamship, sailing ships were the vessels of commerce on the Great Lakes. Courtesy of State of Michigan Archives.

delivered hundreds of thousands of settlers to cities and towns around the state. Michigan's waterways provided resources and transportation for the Midwest's industrial revolution, and today they remain among the busiest shipping routes in the world.

Rivers and streams drain Michigan's forests and farmlands in rushing torrents or in gentle meanders. Inland lakes and wetlands nurture an amazing variety of aquatic life and provide an equally diverse array of recreational opportunities. But it is our sweet inland seas—Lakes Superior, Michigan, Huron, and Erie—that form the heart and soul of our state. The Great Lakes are an indelible part of Michigan's past, and they will be a defining aspect of her future.

Whether your backroad destination is a scenic lighthouse, a small town, a secluded beach, or through the heart of Michigan's wilderness, your travels will take you through a state filled with history and unique beauty. From north to south and from coast to coast, the people of the Wolverine State know, as the state's motto declares, *Si quaeris peninsulam amoenam, circumspice*: "If you seek a pleasant peninsula, look about you."

PART I

PASTIES AND IRON ORE: THE UPPER PENINSULA

FACING PAGE:

A short walk along a raised boardwalk brings visitors to Wagner Falls near Munising. Michigan's Upper Peninsula is home to nearly two hundred waterfalls.

ABOVE:

A blacktop road snakes its way through the forest in Michigan's Keweenaw County. Michigan contains 19 million acres of timberland, covering 51 percent of the state.

Michigan's Upper Peninsula is a geographically and culturally unique corner of the United States. Home to two national forests, three state forests, nearly twenty state parks, and dozens of other natural areas, the UP is an outdoors lover's dream. The UP's northern latitude and its proximity to three of the world's largest lakes create a climate of extremes. Mild and wet summers give way to crisp autumn days, creating perfect conditions for the UP's lush forests to display one of the best fall color shows in the country. Winter brings a heavy blanket of snow that often lasts well into April. Tourist towns that cater to family vacationers in the summer quickly switch gears during the winter to accommodate an ever-growing number of snowmobilers and skiers.

While the climate throughout the UP is generally similar, the geography of the eastern and western portions of the peninsula differs significantly. The low-lying terrain and high water table of the eastern Upper Peninsula favors swamp forests and bog communities such as those found in the Seney National Wildlife Refuge. The western portion of the Upper Peninsula consists of ancient bedrock, often protruding through the soil as rocky outcrops. The Porcupine Mountains and the Keweenaw Peninsula are typical examples of this type of terrain.

The citizens of the UP are a self-dependant and hearty lot who proudly refer to themselves as Yoopers (pronounced YOU-purrs). Many current residents are the descendants of immigrants who left Europe in the mid-nineteenth century for the mines and logging camps of northern Michigan. Others are descendants of Upper Michigan's first native people. Many retirees also enjoy the slow-paced life of the UP.

Good fishing, beautiful scenery, and outdoor recreation are never far away in Michigan's Upper Peninsula. Whether you enjoy a solitary beach and a book, a stream and a fly rod, a hike in the forest, or a visit to an historic town, Michigan's Upper Peninsula awaits you.

Route 1

From the city of Ontonagon, follow State Highway M64 west toward Silver City. In Silver City, follow State Highway M107 west to the park headquarters and visitor center. To visit the Escarpment Overlook and Lake of the Clouds, continue west on Highway M107. To drive along the southern perimeter of Porcupine Mountains Wilderness State Park and to visit the western side of the park, backtrack on Highway M107 to South Boundary Road. Take South Boundary Road to County Road 519 and turn north toward the Presque Isle campground.

Porcupine Mountains Wilderness State Park

Shaped in the rounded posture of a porcupine, with pointed quills made of tall hemlock and hardwood trees, the Porcupine Mountains cover 92 square miles of rugged wilderness in the northwest corner of Michigan's Upper Peninsula. Porcupine Mountains Wilderness State Park is the domain of black bears, bobcats, pine martens, falcons, eagles, wolves, and, some say, cougars. It is also the realm of sightseers, backpackers, downhill and cross-country skiers, sportsmen, and anyone who seeks to experience one of the Midwest's last-remaining true wilderness areas.

By geological standards, the Porcupine Mountains stand just short of being considered true mountains. At 1,958 feet, Summit Peak is the highest point in the Porkies, missing the 2,000-foot standard of a true mountain by a mere 42 feet. This shortfall is less evident along the park's steep trails than it is in the textbook. The scholarly definition is also a moot point when you consider that its mountainous topography probably spared the area from

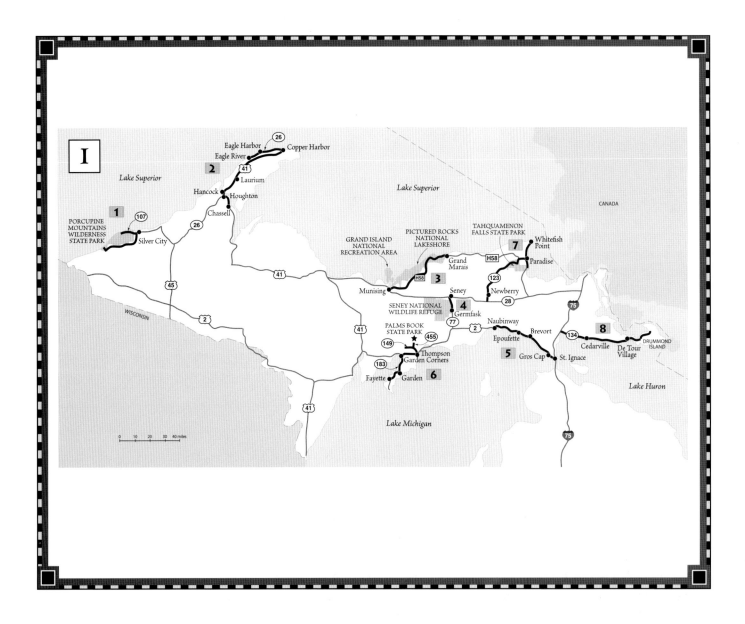

Bunchberry, a diminutive member of the dogwood family, shares the forest floor with club moss in Michigan's Upper Peninsula.

Rainfall generated from nearby Lake Superior keeps the forests in the Porcupine Mountains lush and green in the summer. Boulders, fallen trees, and low areas are covered with bright green moss, providing a wet nursery for a variety of mushrooms.

The Presque Isle River drops over three major waterfalls and a series of scenic rapids as it rushes toward Lake Superior. The view from a swinging bridge over the river shows the jigsaw carving that flowing water has made in the bedrock of the river.

Lake of the Clouds sits nestled in the rolling terrain of Porcupine Mountains Wilderness State Park.

the clear-cut logging that ravaged more accessible forests all over Michigan. Today, one half of Porcupine Mountains Wilderness State Park is still covered by virgin timber.

Human interaction with the Porcupine Mountains began with the earliest woodland people of the Upper Great Lakes, who scoured the rugged terrain for veins of copper. To expose the ore, rocks containing veins of copper were heated over open fires and fractured by immersion in cold water. The malleable metal was then fashioned into tools, arrow points, or jewelry. Copper was a useful material and an important trading commodity for the Great Lakes tribes, and metal from the Porcupine Mountains was traded across the region.

Large-scale mining for copper was attempted by European settlers beginning in 1848, but the expense of getting the ore to market made the endeavor unprofitable. When demand fell after the Civil War, most of the mines were abandoned. One of the last attempts to glean copper from the Porcupine Mountains was made in 1867 with the opening of the Nonesuch Mine. The mine operated sporadically until 1910, producing only 180 tons of refined copper in forty-three years of operation, while gobbling up the fortunes of its investors.

During Michigan's logging boom, timber was cut along the shore of Lake Superior, but logging in the rugged interior of the Porcupine Mountains was limited to cutting hardwood beams to shore up mine shafts. The last logging operation occurred in the park in 1953, after tornado-strength winds blew ashore off Lake Superior near the mouth of the Big Carp River, devastating 1,200 acres of forest. Faced with more than 10 million board feet of lumber lying in twisted piles on the ground, the park superintendent allowed loggers to salvage the wood.

To get acquainted with Porcupine Mountains Wilderness State Park, stop in at the visitor center near the junction of State Highway M107 and South Boundary Road. The visitor center features lifelike displays depicting the park's fauna, flora, and natural history, and a large-scale relief map of the park's terrain. The Visitor Center Nature Trail, a one-mile loop with interpretive stations along the way, will give you a good feel for what the Porcupine Mountains are all about.

From the visitor center, follow Highway M107 west until the road ends at the Escarpment Overlook and Lake of the Clouds. This is the most visited and photographed spot in the park, and with good reason. A trail from the parking area leads to the top of a rocky escarpment, where several viewing platforms have been built. A short stone wall snakes along the edge of a four-hundred-foot precipice, and beyond the wall, the Porcupine Mountains fade to the horizon. Below and to the east, Lake of the Clouds shimmers under the breeze that flows through the Carp River valley. At the western end of Lake of the Clouds, the Carp River cuts a serpentine path through the trees as it begins its nine-mile run to Lake Superior. In the autumn, the crowns of the trees along the valley and in the surrounding hills radiate with red, orange, and yellow leaves.

To view the panorama from a different angle, follow the Escarpment Trail east or west along the top of the cliff. The trail weaves in and out of the woods and onto rocky outcrops overlooking the lake and the valley below. If you feel up to a steep climb, the North Mirror Lake Trail leads down to a bridge crossing the Carp River and then on to Lake of the Clouds.

The parking area for Escarpment Overlook also provides overnight parking for several backcountry trailheads, including Lakeshore Trail, Escarpment Trail, Big Carp River Trail, Lost Lake Trail, and North Mirror Lake Trail, which can all be accessed nearby. On a summer's afternoon, the parking area is abuzz with excited hikers, checking and rechecking their gear before hitting the trails.

The interior of the park is not the exclusive domain of the hardcore backpacker. Sixteen rustic cabins within the park are available by reservation. Each cabin features from two to eight bunks with mattresses, a wood-burning stove, cooking and eating utensils, a table with benches, and an axe and saw for cutting firewood. The cabins range from two to four miles' hiking distance from a parking area. The use of a rowboat is included with the rustic cabins rented on the park's inland lakes. Reservations are handled through the park office.

From Highway M107, backtrack to South Boundary Road and head toward the western end of the park and the Presque Isle River. Along the way, keep your eyes open for wildlife crossing the road or feeding along the shoulder. White-tailed deer, black bear, and coyote commonly make use of this corridor. South Boundary Road crosses several trout streams along the perimeter of the park. Check at the park office for license and catch-limit information.

A short (0.75 mile) trail to Greenstone Falls on the Little Carp River begins at the parking area at the end of Little Carp River Road, 16 miles west of the visitor center off South Boundary Road. The trail follows the banks of the Little Carp River past a small cascade called Overlook Falls, and then descends into the river's gorge via a set of steps. A makeshift bridge cut from a huge fallen tree crosses the river before the trail ascends the opposite riverbank to a junction with the Little Carp River Trail. Follow the Little Carp River Trail west for a short distance to Greenstone Falls. Below the trail in the river's gorge, the Little Carp River cascades in several rivulets onto moss-covered rocks in the riverbed. The muted light filtering through the towering pine trees surrounding Greenstone Falls, and the play of falling water on the dark river stones, gives visitors the sense they are exploring an exotic and primeval place.

The western edge of Porcupine Mountains Wilderness State Park features a semi-modern campground and a breathtaking stretch of rapids and waterfalls on the Presque Isle River. For hikers, the 16-mile-long Lake Superior Trail starts (and ends) here. The much shorter East River and West River trails also start here, following the Presque Isle River from its mouth at Lake Superior to the bridge at South Boundary Road. A swinging bridge crosses the river near Lake Superior, offering a bird's-eye view of the river's

The Big Carp River meanders through a valley of northern hardwood in early autumn. Noted for its population of native brook trout, the Big Carp flows through the Porcupine Mountains from Lake of the Clouds to Lake Superior.

Manido Falls is one of a series of waterfalls on the Presque Isle River in Porcupine Mountains Wilderness State Park. The rapids and waterfalls along the Presque Isle River make it one of the most scenic stretches of river in Michigan.

The cedar-lined Little Carp River flows through a remote and beautiful portion of Porcupine Mountains Wilderness State Park.

impressive rapids, swirling whirlpools, and rippled shale banks. Along the East River and West River trails, on the last mile of its descent into Lake Superior, the Presque Isle River drops more than 100 feet over a series of rapids and cascades.

The real quality that sets Porcupine Mountains Wilderness State Park apart from other parks is the chance for visitors to experience true wilderness—to pass through a forest of cedar trees that were saplings when Lewis and Clark reached the Pacific Ocean, or to run their hands over river rock worn smooth by centuries of unhindered, swift, cold water. To explore the Porcupine Mountains is to brush against a rare world. The park is remote, and many of the trails are strenuous, steep, and challenging, but the rewards are unique, inspiring, and memorable.

THE KEWEENAW PENINSULA: MICHIGAN'S COPPER COUNTRY

ROUTE 2

From Baraga, follow U.S. Highway 41 to Houghton, Hancock, and Calumet. In Calumet, U.S. 41 and State Highway M26 merge and head north toward Copper Harbor. Near Eagle Harbor, Highway M26 splits and heads west toward Eagle Harbor and Lake Superior. To follow the route north along Lake Superior's shore and to reach Brockway Mountain Drive, follow Highway M26 toward Eagle Harbor. To drive along the interior of the Keweenaw Peninsula to Copper Harbor, follow U.S. 41 north to its end at Copper Harbor.

The Keweenaw Peninsula juts into Lake Superior, resolute against the icy waters that shape its climate, its ecology, and its geology. This northernmost coast of Michigan's mainland is far enough removed from the southern part of the state that summer twilight lingers noticeably longer and winter days are regrettably shorter. The Lake Superior weather machine rules here, piling snow to the rooftops in winter and bringing autumn's colors early. Still, the people who live here know, and those who visit agree, that the rugged beauty of the Keweenaw is unmatched anywhere in the state.

Houghton, and its sister city Hancock, sit on opposite sides of Portage Lake, the part-natural, part-manmade waterway that separates the Keweenaw Peninsula from mainland Michigan. Houghton and Hancock are thriving towns filled with historic buildings and with neighborhoods built into the steep hillside along the lake. Houghton, on the south side of the lake, is the larger of the two cities and home to Michigan Technological University, a highly rated engineering school. Hancock is the site of Finlandia University, founded in 1896 by Finnish immigrants who had come to the Keweenaw Peninsula to work in the copper mines.

In contrast to the modern buildings found on the campus of Michigan Tech, many of the historic buildings and churches in Houghton, Hancock, and nearby Calumet are constructed from blocks of distinctive ochre-red stone known as Jacobsville sandstone. Easily carved and structurally strong, Jacobsville sandstone was the building block of choice in northern Michigan during the mining boom of the nineteenth century. A supply of the Precambrian stone near the mouth of the Portage River on Keweenaw Bay was discovered by George Craig in 1861. An emigrant stonecutter from Yorkshire, England, Craig founded a small town at the site of his quarry. His operation was short lived, however, as the larger Jacobsville Quarry, a short distance away, soon became the principal supplier of the stone, as well as its namesake.

Horses and mules were used to haul trams loaded with ore in many of Michigan's early copper and iron mines. Courtesy of State of Michigan Archives/negative #6639

An artist's rendition of a visit to the Ontonagon Boulder, a boulder of pure copper found lying on the banks of the Ontonagon River near the Keweenaw Peninsula. The boulder helped fuel a mining rush in the nineteenth century that transformed the area from wilderness to a multi-ethnic metropolis. Courtesy of State of Michigan Archives.

FACING PAGE:
Lichen-encrusted bedrock and agate beaches line the shore of Lake Superior between Eagle Harbor and Copper Harbor on the Keweenaw Peninsula.

TOP LEFT:
The last rays of sunset highlight the waves and rocks along the west coast of the Keweenaw.

BOTTOM LEFT:
The Quincy copper mine north of Hancock is part of the Keweenaw National Historical Park, a system of public and private parks on the Keweenaw Peninsula dedicated to preserving the copper-mining heritage of the region.

BOTTOM RIGHT:
The Douglas House in downtown Houghton is one of dozens of interesting and historic buildings found on the Keweenaw Peninsula.

In Calumet, U.S. Highway 41 joins State Highway M26 and passes north through the rugged interior of the Keweenaw Peninsula. When Highway M26 splits to the west toward Eagle River, three possible routes to Copper Harbor present themselves: U.S. 41 north, Highway M26 to Eagle River and then north along Lake Superior's shore, or Highway M26 to Brockway Mountain Drive, which loops over Brockway Mountain and rejoins Highway M26 just outside Copper Harbor. Each route is unique and beautiful in its own way, and if time allows, each is well worth experiencing.

The trip up the Keweenaw Peninsula ends with U.S. 41 at Copper Harbor and Fort Wilkins State Park. On the map, Copper Harbor looks to be an out-of-the-way destination, but this town at the tip of the Keweenaw draws a surprising number of campers and tourists. Many of the travelers who visit Copper Harbor are bound for Isle Royale National Park aboard the *Isle Royale Queen IV*, a one-hundred-passenger ship that sails from Copper Harbor every day except Wednesday during the summer months. Other visitors come to Copper Harbor to see Fort Wilkins, an 1840s-era army post built to keep the peace among settlers in the mining community. At Fort Wilkins, interpreters in period dress sit outside authentically furnished buildings, spinning tales from the mid-1800s.

Douglas Houghton, Michigan's first state geologist and the namesake of the city of Houghton, saw many memorable sights during his journeys around the Great Lakes in the mid-nineteenth century. But Houghton's scientific mind reeled when, during a geological expedition in 1830, the legendary Ontonagon Boulder finally stood before him. Tales of a boulder of pure copper lying on the banks of the Ontonagon River had been told and retold, since the times of the Jesuit explorers two centuries earlier. The boulder had been visited by traders and statesmen, from the British entrepreneur Alexander Henry to Michigan's first territorial governor, General Lewis Cass. Now Houghton wondered if this 3,700-pound chunk of copper was evidence of a great wealth of minerals in the wild country of western Lake Superior. As it turns out, it was.

Despite Houghton's doubts a rush to discover and extract copper from the region was soon underway. Between the first onslaught of prospectors in 1843 and the heyday of mining at the end of the nineteenth century, the Keweenaw Peninsula was transformed from a wilderness into a multiethnic metropolis. Towns sprung up all along the Keweenaw at the sites of mines, smelters, and stamp mills. (The stamp mills crushed the copper ore and separated out the copper.) By 1890, the city of Calumet, at the site of the Calumet and Hecla Mine, had a population of over 60,000 people. The ethnic diversity of the town was reflected in its institutions. With thirty-three churches, thirty schools, five theaters, and sixty saloons, Calumet's immigrant populations built cultural enclaves within the city's larger community.

Copper mining on the peninsula is largely a thing of the past, but the lure and history of the mines still play a key role in the area's economy. Just north of Hancock, the National Park Service has preserved the remnants of the Quincy Mine as part of the Keweenaw National Historic Park. The Quincy

Mine site offers tours of the former copper-mining facilities, including an underground excursion 400 feet into the mine.

As for the fate of the Ontonagon Boulder, it was purchased in 1841 by Julius Eldred of Detroit from Chief O-Kun-De-Kun of the Ontonagon Chippewa. Eldred paid the chief $150 for the boulder: $45 in cash and the rest in goods from his Detroit hardware store. Unfortunately for Eldred, someone else had claimed the land where the boulder lay. To regain his prize, he was forced to pay the landowner an additional $1,365.

Eldred's problems were not over yet. To remove the boulder from its remote location, Eldred hired a crew of twenty-one men to cut a 4.5-mile-long path through the dense forest and haul the rock out on a portable, sectional rail line. While Eldred struggled to get the boulder to Detroit, the United States Secretary of War, James M. Porter, claimed eminent domain over the famous copper boulder and ordered it seized. Eldred was allowed to bring the boulder to Detroit and display it for several weeks in October 1843. The boulder was then shipped to Washington, D.C. for display at the Smithsonian Institution, where it remains today.

Railroads brought the raw ore from Michigan's copper and iron mines to ports along Lake Superior where it was shipped to foundries on the southern Great Lakes. Courtesy of State of Michigan Archives/negative #06881

RIGHT:
Fort Wilkins State Park in Copper Harbor features a frontier army outpost and a large campground. Built in 1844, the fort was established to keep the peace in the rowdy mining towns of the Keweenaw.

BELOW:
The lighthouse at Eagle Harbor is part of a maritime history museum complex operated by the Keweenaw Historical Society.

ABOVE:
Beachcombing along Lake Superior is a favorite pastime along the pebble beaches of the Keweenaw Peninsula. Rock hounds search the beach for agates, fossils, and colorful pieces of quartz.

LEFT:
A scenic trail leads from Canyon Falls Roadside Park on U.S. Highway 41 to Canyon Falls, where the Sturgeon River drops in a rushing torrent into a deep canyon.

PICTURED ROCKS NATIONAL LAKESHORE

ROUTE 3

From State Highway M28 in Munising, follow County Road H58 east toward Grand Marais. Miners Castle, Chapel Rock, and Beaver Basin side routes are noted earlier in this text.

The city of Munising sits snug on the shore of Munising Bay on Lake Superior, separated from the dangerous moods of the big lake by Grand Island, which sits at the mouth of the bay. Surrounding the city is some of the prettiest country in Michigan. To the west, alternating sand and stone beaches extend to Marquette. To the south, the waterfalls and rolling wooded hills of Hiawatha National Forest stretch all the way to Bay de Noc on Lake Michigan. To the east, Pictured Rocks National Lakeshore protects 40 miles of spectacular Superior shoreline.

Munising thrived as a logging center during the logging boom of the late nineteenth and early twentieth centuries. Like many northern Michigan communities that fell on hard times when the logging industry waned, Munising's population has fluctuated through the years. Nonetheless, with a paper-products plant, a sawmill, a planer mill, and a veneer mill all nearby, the forestry industry remains an important component of Munising's economy.

With the rise in automobile-based tourism and the establishment of Pictured Rocks National Lakeshore, Munising's economy has shifted to accommodate the influx of urban vacationers. An abundance of motels, restaurants, campgrounds, resorts, and other tourist services cater to the large number of visitors the city receives each year. Snowmobiling, summer sightseeing, autumn-color touring, fishing, and hunting make Munising a year-round destination.

While there is plenty to see in and about the city of Munising, our route follows County Road H58 east through Pictured Rocks National Lakeshore to Grand Marais. Alternating between blacktop and gravel along the way, County Road H58 is the main access to the many points of interest along the national lakeshore. Most of the road is left unplowed in the winter, but is well maintained the remainder of the year. It is a good idea to pick up a detailed map at the park headquarters at Sand Point before your trip. The side roads on our route are well marked, but many other roads lack signage. A compass is also very handy.

The Pictured Rocks were set aside as a national treasure only recently, but travelers have long marveled at the colorful and intricate sandstone cliffs of this stretch of Superior's shore. Henry Rowe Schoolcraft—a historian, geologist, and explorer—wrote in 1820: "We had been told of the variety in the color and form of these rocks, but were wholly unprepared to encounter the surprising groups of overhanging precipices, towering walls, caverns and waterfalls . . . mingled in the most wonderful disorder." Long before Schoolcraft, the Native Americans who inhabited the region held the carved and colorful rock formations as examples of the Creator's artistry.

The Miners Castle area is the first place to get an appreciation of the beauty and the immense scale of the Pictured Rocks. From H58, take Miners Castle Road north toward the cliffs. Along the way the road passes through a thick forest of sugar maple and over the Miners River. For an interesting side trip, take an hour or so and stop at Miners Falls. The 1.2-mile round-trip follows an easily walked gravel footpath through a beautiful forest to a series of wooden decks overlooking the falls. Here the water of the Miners River plummets 30 feet or so before sliding down a wide chute of black rock. Over the years, the cascading water has carved the stone of the riverbed into fanciful designs and patterns.

As you near the lakeshore on Miners Castle Road, follow the signs for Miners Castle to a large, paved parking lot. A short walk past several interpretive exhibits takes you to a platform at the edge of the precipice. What you see before you is bedrock formed 500 million years ago during the late-Precambrian and Cambrian periods. The ancient rocks were reexposed about ten thousand years ago as the Wisconsin Glacier retreated. The fantastic shapes, grottos, and intricate carvings on the vertical rock walls are the result of centuries of battering waves and ice. Iron, copper, manganese, and other minerals seeping through the porous sandstone give the cliffs their warm colors.

The main attraction here is the monolithic Miners Castle, a castlelike rock formation standing nine stories tall and extending out into Lake Superior. Two rock "turrets" top the castle walls like the weathered guard posts of an ancient Scottish fortress. To the west you can see a portion of Grand Island National Recreation Area at the mouth of Munising Bay. A paved trail begins at the viewing platform and leads along the cliff to several different vantage points.

Viewing the cliffs in a watercraft is a great way to appreciate why the Pictured Rocks were selected as the nation's first national lakeshore. Miners Castle is a favorite destination for kayakers, who can put in at Sand Point or at nearby Miners Beach. Lake Superior, it should be remembered, is a large, cold, and dangerous body of water, prone to sudden squalls and large waves. Inexperienced paddlers can join supervised kayaking trips offered by several outfitters in Munising. For those who prefer to sightsee from the comfort of a ship's deck, a charter boat company in Munising offers tours of the Pictured Rocks aboard a large passenger boat.

For another up-close look at the colorful rocks, or if you'd like to do a bit of beachcombing, backtrack down Miners Castle Road and follow signs leading to Miners Beach. From the parking area, several trails lead through a forest of pines and lichen down to the mile-long beach. At either end of Miners Beach, the sandstone cliffs rise slowly from the sand toward the sky. From the eastern side of the beach, you can access the Lakeshore Trail, which extends for over 40 miles along the cliffs and shoreline of Lake Superior. A (careful) walk along the Lakeshore Trail unveils one spectacular panorama after another, as the trail winds along the top of 50- to 200-foot-tall cliffs.

The next leg of the journey leads to the Chapel Rock area, about 9 miles east of Miners Castle Road on County Road H58. From the intersection of County Road H58 and County Road 639, follow the signs to the Chapel parking area. From there, you can choose between a 3-mile round-trip hike to Chapel Falls and a more ambitious 9-mile loop that leads to Chapel Beach, Chapel Rock, and Grand Portal Point.

Michigan's Upper Peninsula is renowned for its autumn color. From late September until mid-October colorful leaves adorn the trees and carpet the forest floor.

FACING PAGE:
Evening light brings a warm glow to the sculpted sandstone of Pictured Rocks National Lakeshore.

ABOVE:
The paper birch was an important tree to the native people of Michigan. Its waterproof white bark was used for canoes, kettles, and shelters.

The trail to Chapel Falls is steep at times, but it is wide and well maintained. Just before you reach the falls, the trail crosses a wooden bridge over the gurgling waters of Section Creek. A few hundred feet farther brings you to a viewing platform, built on the edge of a bowl-shaped canyon facing Chapel Falls. The water from Section Creek seems to pour from a dark hole in the forest and slides in an ever-widening path down the dark rock face. The cascade is framed by trees growing up from the bottom of the canyon.

East of the Chapel area is the Beaver Basin area and Little and Big Beaver lakes. The heavily wooded Beaver Basin comprises the widest point of Pictured Rocks National Lakeshore. For a great panoramic view of the area, watch for the side road off County Road H58 to the Beaver Basin Overlook. Another side road leads to the drive-in campground at Little Beaver Lake. From a parking area just outside the campground at Little Beaver, you can access a trail that leads around Little Beaver and Big Beaver lakes, or you can follow a fork that leads down to Twelve Mile Beach and the Lakeshore Trail on Lake Superior.

A few miles beyond the Beaver Basin area, County Road H58 takes a sharp turn to the north and into the Kingston Plains. The Kingston Plains is a strangely beautiful area of massive, ancient tree stumps covered in lichen. The often blackened stumps are all that is left of a forest of white pine that was logged at the end of the nineteenth century. Over the years, forest fires swept through the plains, burning the lumbermen's slashings and the remaining stumps. Recently, fire suppression has allowed some regrowth, but the twisted stumps remain as a reminder of the lasting effects of poor forestry practices.

At Twelve Mile Beach Campground, County Road H58 passes through a forest of graceful paper birch. This fast-growing, shade-intolerant, fire-dependent tree was used extensively by the Native Americans of the region for canoes, shelter, and utensils. The drive-in campground has few amenities, but what it lacks in comforts, it makes up for in beauty. Along Lake Superior's shore, driftwood-strewn Twelve Mile Beach stretches to the horizon. From the campground, a 2-mile-long, self-guided trail leads through a variety of upland forest communities, including the paper-birch forest. In the autumn, when the trees' crown of leaves turns gold and their slender trunks sway under a lake breeze, a walk through the birch trees is pure magic.

The final leg of our journey through the Pictured Rocks takes us to the Grand Sable Dunes. Covering 5 square miles and perched atop high sand bluffs overlooking Lake Superior, the windswept dunes are another beautiful and unusual feature of this national lakeshore. For a great panoramic view of the Grand Sable Banks and Dunes, take the short trail to the Log Slide Overlook. Accounts from the era when the wooden log chute was operated tell of the chute catching fire from the tremendous friction generated by the sliding logs. The wooden chute has been removed, but it is still easy to imagine the cacophony produced as the huge logs slid down the wooden chute and into Lake Superior. Stop by the Grand Sable Visitor Center for an in-depth look at the history and ecology of the dunes.

SENEY NATIONAL WILDLIFE REFUGE

Seney is a town with a reputation. At least that was the case in the 1880s, when the small hamlet became the center of the logging industry in the eastern Upper Peninsula. Street brawls and gambling, murder and prostitution, and a reckless disregard for law and order prevailed in the town at the time. The Seney of yesteryear was living proof that the rowdy cowboys of the Wild West had nothing on Michigan's lumberjacks. When the hardworking loggers poured into Seney from the surrounding lumber camps on Saturday night to spend their pay, they had over a dozen saloons and several brothels from which to choose, and only one church to redeem them on Sunday morning.

Things around the town of Seney had settled down considerably by the time Ernest Hemingway visited in 1919 to fish for trout on the Fox River. Fresh from the carnage of World War I and still limping from his wounds, Hemingway and two friends traveled from Petoskey, Michigan, for a bit of adventure in the far north. Hemingway's experiences that August on the Fox River form the basis for his short story "Big Two-Hearted River." Poetic license is thought to be the reason Hemingway chose the nearby Two-Hearted River for the story's title instead of the Fox River, although he may have been protecting his favorite fishing hole, like any good fisherman.

Small hotels, restaurants, a grocery store, and a couple hundred friendly residents make the town of Seney a great base from which to explore the surrounding countryside. Located at the intersection of State Highway M77, State Highway M28, and the Fox River, the town is a year-round destination for travelers seeking to recreate in the north country. Laced with wild rivers and dotted with hundreds of lakes, the nearby Superior State Forest and Hiawatha National Forest draw fishermen, hunters, hikers, campers, snowmobilers, and nature lovers from around the country.

The crown jewel in the midst of the natural splendor that surrounds the town is its namesake wildlife refuge, located south and west of town. The 95,455-acre Seney National Wildlife Refuge is a watery oasis for northern plants and wildlife, including some of the rarest animals and birds in Michigan. The refuge is a model of successful land reclamation and management that began in 1935 and continues today.

Stripped of its mature trees, scorched by wildfires, and drained for farmland, most of the refuge's wilderness lay in ruin at the beginning of the twentieth century. After the loggers moved on and the poor soil and harsh climate drove farmers to seek tillable earth elsewhere, the abandoned land slowly reverted to state ownership. In the 1930s the Civilian Conservation Corps and several other Depression-era government agencies set to work to restore Seney.

The first task the renovators faced was to reverse the drainage system put in place by a development company to produce farmland from the water-saturated soil. A series of dikes and ditches were created to form twenty-one large ponds and over 7,000 acres of open water. Access roads and service

ROUTE 4

From State Highway M28 in the town of Seney, follow State Highway M77 south toward Germfask and Seney National Wildlife Refuge. The Marshlands Wildlife Drive begins at the refuge visitor center.

RIGHT:
Trapped and hunted to near extinction for its soft fur, the beaver has made a strong comeback and is once again a common sight in Michigan, especially in the wetlands of Seney National Wildlife Refuge.

BELOW:
Mist rises into the air on a cool October morning in the Seney National Wildlife Refuge.

ABOVE:

A wingspan of nearly eight feet and an adult weight of up to 35 pounds make the trumpeter swan the world's largest waterfowl. The shallow pools of the Seney National Wildlife Refuge provide an excellent habitat for the swans, which build five-foot-wide nests of cattails and grass, often atop an abandoned muskrat lodge.

LEFT:

Fallen and dead trees provide a nursery for a host of seedlings, mosses, lichen, and flowering plants such as this wintergreen.

roads were built to maintain the system and allow the public to enjoy the large number of waterfowl that found the protected pools a good place to raise their young. In 1935, a small flock of Canada geese were released in the new sanctuary and allowed to migrate that winter. To the delight of many, the geese returned to the sanctuary's ponds the following spring and nested. Within ten years, Canada geese were thriving once again in Seney.

Two hundred different species of birds have been recorded in Seney, and often a pair of binoculars or a spotting scope is all that is needed to find a dozen species floating on a pond or flitting through the trees. Many of Michigan's large mammals also find a home in the vast wilderness of Seney. The timber wolf and the black bear live here, as do the white-tailed deer, otter, red fox, beaver, muskrat, and coyote. In all, fifty species of mammals have been found in the refuge.

To explore Seney National Wildlife Refuge by automobile, follow Highway M77 south from the town of Seney for about 5 miles to the visitor center entrance on the west side of the road. The visitor center is open from 9:00 AM to 5:00 PM, from May 15 through October 15. The building is home to many interesting exhibits on the animals, plants, ecology, and management of the refuge. Be sure to drive slowly in the center's parking lot and watch your step: a welcoming committee of Canada geese spends the summer lounging and greeting guests around the visitor center.

The Marshlands Wildlife Drive—a 7-mile-long, one-way gravel road through the eastern portion of the refuge—begins near the visitor center. The narrow road winds past many of the reserve's pools, along the edges of large wetlands, and through upland forests carpeted with blueberry bushes. Opportunities to view wildlife are plentiful along this road, especially during the first and last light of the day, when the animals and birds are most active. Small parking areas, pull-offs, and viewing platforms are strategically placed along the road at locations where wildlife viewing is particularly good. Along the edge of one of the larger ponds, a spotting scope is provided to view a bald eagle's nest on the opposite shore. Marshlands Wildlife Drive reconnects with Highway M77 a short distance south of the visitor center entrance.

The small town of Germfask, located about 3 miles south of the visitor center, is a good place to grab a bite to eat or to continue your Seney adventure via canoe along the Manistique River. A campground and canoe livery in town rents canoes and provides return transportation for trips along the easily paddled Manistique River.

Remote areas of the refuge are accessible to hikers, mountain bikers, skiers, and snowshoers via a network of trails and fire roads. Access to some areas may be limited at certain times of the year to protect plants and breeding birds, so check at the visitor center for current trail restrictions. In the spring and early summer, be sure to bring protection from biting insects when hiking in Seney. The numerous mosquitoes and black flies can ruin the wilderness experience for an unprepared visitor.

The town of Seney was the center of lumbering operations in the eastern Upper Peninsula during the days of the logging boom. Many of the town's buildings were built on stilts because of the flooding caused by the deforestation around the town. Courtesy of State of Michigan Archives/negative # 17504

Seney National Wildlife Refuge is also home to a unique natural feature known as the Strangmoor Bog. Located deep within the refuge's wilderness zone, the Strangmoor is an area of low, parallel, sandy ridges separated by wet troughs. It is the product of glacial deposition and the prevailing winds, which sculpted the low hills. This unusual geological formation has been named a registered national landmark. Because of its remoteness, the Strangmoor is home to many of Seney's larger predators, such as the timber wolf, black bear, and bobcat, which require expansive territories and minimal human interference to thrive.

Seney's beauty lies not in dramatic landscape but in the subtle splendor of a fertile ecosystem in its prime. If you enjoy a place where each turn of the road brings a new chance to encounter wildlife in its natural surroundings, and if you appreciate the diversity of life that only a wetland can produce, then Seney National Wildlife Refuge awaits you.

US 2, St. Ignace to Naubinway

When Father Jacques Marquette landed on the northern shore of the Straits of Mackinac in 1671 to build St. Ignace Mission, he could never have imagined the changes that the next few centuries would bring to this remote village of the Huron people. His mission would grow into an important trading center and military outpost, and eventually would become the gateway to Michigan's Upper Peninsula. Marquette's evangelical passion would propel him into the unexplored reaches of North America and indelibly join his name with early European discovery in the New World. In nine short years, from 1666

ROUTE 5

From Interstate 75 in St. Ignace, follow U.S. Highway 2 west to Naubinway.

LEFT:
Dune grass and a snow fence keep the shifting sands of Lake Michigan's beach in check.

ABOVE:
Beach stones are rounded and polished by the surf of Lake Michigan.

until his death in 1675, Marquette explored large areas of the Great Lakes, mastered several native languages, and together with Louis Joliet, mapped the Mississippi River.

Straits State Park is home to the Father Marquette National Memorial, a testament to the missionary and explorer who is said to have genuinely cared about the native people he encountered. The memorial is located on a rise overlooking the Straits of Mackinac. The site of Marquette's original mission at St. Ignace is now the home of the Museum of Ojibwa Culture at Marquette Mission Park.

As you move west along U.S. Highway 2 out of St. Ignace, the hotels and restaurants begin to thin out and are soon replaced by sweeping views of Lake Michigan. In addition to its scenic turnouts, picnic areas, and state-forest campgrounds, U.S. 2 is best known for the miles of sandy beach found along the roadside. On a sunny summer day, swimmers, sunbathers, beachcombers, and lawn-chair loungers park along the roadside and find a private place in the sun. Access to the beach is often just a short walk from the road or down a flight of stairs from the parking area of a scenic turnout or picnic site.

Low sand dunes lie between U.S. 2 and Lake Michigan along some portions of the route. In these areas, access to the beach may be restricted at certain times of the year to protect the nesting grounds of one of Michigan's rarest birds, the piping plover. Listed as an endangered species in Michigan and as threatened throughout much of its North American range, the piping plover prefers to nest on wide, sandy beaches with little vegetation. Unfortunately, people also like to use these areas for recreation, especially during the plover's critical nesting months of July and August.

A few miles inland from U.S. 2 and the Lake Michigan shoreline, just east of the town of Brevoort, is one of Michigan's premier big-game fishing holes, Brevoort Lake. During the summer months, anglers ply Brevoort's 4,200 acres of shallow, weedy waters for bass, crappie, walleye, northern pike, and panfish; but in early June, most anglers set their sights on bigger game, the spotted muskellunge.

Lightning-fast reflexes; an oversized mouth full of stout, razor-sharp teeth; and its large size (up to 60 pounds) make the spotted muskellunge, or muskie, a formidable predator. The muskie feeds primarily on other fish, but an occasional duckling or muskrat has been known to disappear from the water's surface in a toothy splash. Muskellunge fishing is not a fast-action sport. Most successful muskie fishermen troll the shallow, muddy flats of Brevoort Lake with flashy metal spoons, hoping to entice a spawning fish to strike. When a muskie does slam into the lure, the ensuing battle between fisherman and fish is a memorable experience.

With thousands of miles of rivers and streams crisscrossing the landscape, Michigan is a state with an abundance of bridges. One of the more picturesque river crossings in the state is over the Cut River as it flows beneath U.S. 2 and into Lake Michigan. Built in 1947, the 641-foot-long Cut River Bridge is one of only two cantilevered-deck truss bridges in Michigan. A popular roadside park next to the bridge has a series of stairs leading to the bottom of the Cut River Gorge allowing several different viewing angles of the bridge along the way. There is a pedestrian walk on the bridge itself, although it is a bit unnerving when a truck or RV rumbles by a few feet away and the deck of the bridge shakes under your feet.

At the western edge of the route along U.S. 2 is the largest commercial fishing port on Lake Michigan, the town of Naubinway. If you have a taste for fresh Lake Michigan fish, then head toward the town's dock in the evening and wait for Naubinway's fishing fleet to return home for the day. Fresh fish can be purchased right off the boat or from merchants in town, who also sell smoked trout and salmon.

Like many northern Michigan towns, Naubinway got its start during the lumber boom of the nineteenth century. The town's excellent natural harbor saved it from the fate of many other Michigan lumber towns by providing safe mooring for a large fishing fleet. Set against a backdrop of sandy Lake Michigan beaches and the Hiawatha National Forest, Naubinway is a place of beauty.

WHAT IS A PASTY?

As you travel along U.S. 2, or anywhere else in Michigan's Upper Peninsula, you are sure to encounter a roadside restaurant advertising pasties. The pasty has become an icon of the UP, just as fudge has for Mackinac or automobiles have for Detroit. First brought to the new world by Cornish miners, who had left their homeland to work Michigan's copper mines, the pasty is a totally portable, hearty meal that immediately became a staple for miners of all ethnic backgrounds.

The original recipe for the pasty has changed over time to fit the tastes of different ethnic groups and, lately, to match health-conscious eating habits. (Early recipes called for plenty of lard.) In its most basic form, the pasty is similar to a fruit turnover, except that inside the piecrust shell are meat, potatoes, and onions. Other root crops, such as rutabaga or carrots; different spices; and different cuts of meat have been substituted or added as the pasty has evolved into a multicultural food.

Although most people use a knife and fork to eat their pasty, tradition calls for holding the pasty upright in your hands by one corner while eating from the other corner. This eating method not only eliminated the need for carrying a plate and utensils into the mine, but also kept the pasty's juices from spilling out. Pasties were usually baked just before the miner left for work, to ensure they would remain warm until the meal break.

It was tradition to discard the corner of the pasty that had been held, instead of eating it. The uneaten corner was said to be a peace offering to the gremlins that inhabited the mines, but the tradition may have had more to do with the type of mines the Cornish had worked in before emigrating to the UP. In England, the Cornish had worked the tin mines, known to contain large amounts of arsenic. By discarding the portion of the pasty that the miner had held with his hand, he was less likely to ingest the toxic metal.

RIGHT:
A series of walkways, paths, and viewing platforms allow visitors to view the Cut River Bridge on U.S. Highway 2 from many different angles.

BELOW:
A summer thunderstorm darkens the horizon over Lake Michigan.

FACING PAGE:
US Highway 2 follows the northern shore of Lake Michigan from St. Ignace to Naubinway.

ROUTE 6

From U.S. 2 east of Rapid River, take State Highway M183 north toward the town of Garden to Fayette State Park. To visit the Thompson Fish Hatchery, follow U.S. 2 east to Thompson, and then take State Highway M149 north to the hatchery. Continue on Highway M149 north to County Road 442, and turn west and then north on County Road 455 to visit Palms Book State Park. The route to the park is clearly marked.

If you like stories about rum runners and buried treasure, or if you enjoy a morning of world-class fishing followed by a stroll through a ghost town in the afternoon, then cancel your Caribbean cruise and head to the Garden Peninsula and Bay de Noc. The Garden Peninsula sits at the top of Lake Michigan, across Green Bay from Wisconsin's Door County. Bay de Noc is a deepwater sanctuary surrounded by the wetlands and woods of Hiawatha National Forest. This is a land of big water and remote forests, known best to sportsmen and vacationers looking for a quiet corner of Michigan to enjoy.

The ghost town of Fayette sits nestled at the base of Snail Shell Harbor on a small peninsula curving out into Big Bay de Noc. If not for the ruins of the huge blast furnaces and the dormant stacks of the charcoal kilns, it could be just another peaceful corner of northern Michigan. The quite rustle of maple and birch leaves and the fresh lake breeze make the Fayette of the late nineteenth century hard to imagine, but from 1867 until 1891 this isolated settlement was home to one of the busiest iron-smelting operations in Michigan.

To cut the cost of shipping large quantities of impure UP iron ore to smelters in Chicago, the Jackson Iron Company sent Fayette Brown on a mission. He was to find a place with plenty of hardwood trees and a good supply of limestone—two necessary ingredients for turning iron ore into pig iron. A deepwater harbor was necessary to transport the iron ore in and to ship the pig iron out. The site that Fayette Brown chose on Snail Shell Harbor fit the bill perfectly.

Panoramic View, Fayette, Mich.

For nearly twenty-five years, until the hardwood forests were gone and iron-smelting technology changed, the town of Fayette produced pig iron. Fayette was a company town in the sense that all its residents worked for Jackson Iron Company, bought food and goods at the company store, and lived in housing provided by the company. Most residents were completely satisfied with this arrangement, and despite the dirty work, many considered Fayette to be heaven on earth.

In the 1870s, at the height of Fayette's prosperity, the state of Michigan passed the Dry Act, a precursor to the national Prohibition Act of the 1920s. The Jackson Iron Company tried its best to keep liquor out of Fayette, but rum runners from across the lake in Green Bay, Wisconsin, kept the supply line open.

An establishment named the Hole in the Ground Saloon, located a couple of miles outside Fayette, managed to do a brisk business despite the law. The saloon's owner, Alph Berlanquette, is thought to have made a fortune selling bootleg liquor. Berlanquette never put his money in a bank, so upon his death, a treasure hunt ensued for the missing profits of the Hole in the Ground Saloon. Rumors that the ill-gotten profits had been found in 1910 were never proven.

The sordid tale of the Hole in the Ground Saloon does not end with the death of Berlanquette. A shady character named Jim Summers took over the saloon and converted it into a brothel. When a young girl escaped from the brothel and told her story of being held there against her will, an angry mob of townspeople descended on the establishment, burning it to the ground and pummeling Jim Summers and his cohorts. After that night, Jim Summers was never again seen in Fayette.

Fayette was well on its way to becoming a ghost town when this photograph was taken in 1900. During its heyday, the town of Fayette produced pig iron from raw iron ore. Courtesy of State of Michigan Archives/negative #05107

The broken pilings around Snail Shell Harbor once supported a busy dock where waiting ships were loaded with pig iron from Fayette's smelting operations.

ABOVE, LEFT:
A self-operated observation raft allows visitors to view the underwater features in the Kitch-iti-kipi spring, the largest spring in Michigan.

RIGHT:
The window of the former Jackson Iron Company store look out over the quiet waters of Snail Shell Harbor.

FACING PAGE:
The white cliffs along Bay de Noc are made of limestone, which was used in the smelting operations of Fayette to turn iron ore into pig iron.

The furnace crew from the Jackson Iron Company's smelter in Fayette poses in front of the smelter. Despite the dirty work, many townspeople considered Fayette a great place to live. Courtesy of State of Michigan Archives/negative #14493

Along U.S. 2 and State Highway M149 is the Thompson State Fish Hatchery, a facility that raises fish for planting in both the Great Lakes and in Michigan's inland lakes. Several species of salmon and trout, as well as walleye and northern muskellunge are reared in the hatchery's indoor and outdoor tanks. Optimal thermal conditions for each fish pond are maintained by mixing cold spring water with warmer water from a geothermal well. In 2000 and 2001, over 11 million fish from the hatchery were stocked in Michigan waters.

One cannot fault John Bellaire for promoting the legends of Kitch-iti-kipi, even though he later confessed he had made up the stories. Bellaire had come to Manistique from Seney in the 1920s to open a business, and he soon found himself spellbound by the beauty of a nearby natural spring called the Big Spring. Even though the clear water was clogged with debris from a nearby lumber company, Bellaire was able to envision the beauty of the spring in its natural state. Working with the Palms Book Land Company, in 1926 Bellaire arranged for the sale of the land surrounding the Big Spring to the State of Michigan for $10, with the stipulation that the land be used as a public park.

Bellaire was always willing to bring visitors to the site and always anxious to promote the spring as a tourist stop. To this end, he and a cohort concocted a Native American legend that named the spring Kitch-iti-kipi after a young chieftain who died in its icy waters while trying to win the affection of a young maiden. Other legends claimed that a mixture of honey, birch bark, and water from the spring was a surefire love potion. Whatever his intentions, it's clear that Bellaire truly loved the Big Spring, and he would be happy to know that his gift to the people of Michigan still inspires awe in visitors.

Located within the 308-acre Palms Book State Park, the Big Spring is a bowl of acid-clear spring water 200 feet across and 40 feet deep. Beneath the water on the spring's sloping banks lie the skeletons of fallen trees, encrusted with a copper patina of lime. At the bottom of the pool, behind a pane of transparent water, sand boils as 10,000 gallons of spring water flow into the pond each minute. Enormous trout slowly cruise the pool, rising occasionally to pick an insect off the water's surface. To enhance the visitor's experience, the Civilian Conservation Corps constructed a hand-operated raft that traverses the pool.

PARADISE AND BEYOND: TAHQUAMENON FALLS STATE PARK AND WHITEFISH BAY

East of the headwaters of the Tahquamenon River and surrounded by the Lake Superior State Forest, the town of Newberry stands as the gateway to the land of Henry Wadsworth Longfellow's Hiawatha. From its beginnings as the logging headquarters of the Vulcan Furnace Company, Newberry grew to become the county seat when Luce County was formed in 1887 from portions of Chippewa and Mackinaw counties. Today, small businesses and tourist trade provide a living for the town's two thousand residents.

ROUTE 7

From Newberry, follow State Highway M123 north toward Paradise. In Paradise, follow Whitefish Point Road north to Whitefish Point.

Before the smokestacks of the Vulcan Furnace Company brought the industrial revolution to the Newberry area, and before the loggers and farmers arrived, the Chippewa traversed the Tahquamenon watershed in birchbark canoes. In rich wetlands, forests, and rivers, the Chippewa harvested fish and fowl, cranberries, blueberries, and big game. Later, when the fur trade was expanding into northern Michigan, beaver, mink, muskrat, and fox pelts became the staples of commerce in the region. Wild animals, birds, fish, and all the other natural resources of the northern forests still abound around Newberry, and they still attract visitors who love the natural world.

From the city of Newberry, follow State Highway M123 north past Four Mile Corner and then northeast through the Lake Superior State Forest. The heavily wooded landscape along the route is punctuated with glacial-remnant kettle lakes. The lakes are surrounded by vast wetlands filled with wild cranberry and leather leaf. Access roads off Highway M123 lead to the Two-Hearted River and to many remote and beautiful lakes within the state forest.

As you near the eastern edge of Luce County, the Lake Superior State Forest ends and Tahquamenon Falls State Park begins. At 40,000 acres, Tahquamenon Falls State Park is the second-largest state park in Michigan. Most of the park's land is undeveloped, providing the perfect backdrop for year-round wilderness activities, such as hiking, backpacking, camping, fish-

Standing at the entrance to Whitefish Bay since 1849, the Whitefish Point Lighthouse provides guidance for ships passing one of the most dangerous coastlines on the Great Lakes.

LEFT:
Before the Whitefish Point Lighthouse was automated in 1970, members of the U.S. Coast Guard maintained the light and the surrounding grounds. Buildings that once housed the resident keepers are now part of a historical museum.

BELOW:
Dawn colors the clouds pink over the forests of Tahquamenon State Park.

ing, photography, snowmobiling, snowshoeing, and cross-country skiing. The main attraction at the park is Upper Tahquamenon Falls, the second-largest waterfall east of the Mississippi River.

Stretching 200 feet from bank to bank, Upper Tahquamenon Falls spills up to 50,000 gallons of water *per second* in a thunderous cascade over a 50-foot-high cliff. The trademark root-beer-colored water is stained by tannins, leached from cedar, spruce, and hemlock roots in the river's 820-square-mile watershed. A blacktop trail leads from the parking area to the falls, and then along the top of the river's gorge to several overlooks. Visit in the autumn to see the falls framed by the yellow and red leaves of the American beech and the sugar maples. In winter, towering ice columns form on the sides of the cascade, and enormous sheets of ice, carried over the falls by the river's current, shatter in the torrent like great panes of glass.

Four miles downstream of the upper falls is Lower Tahquamenon Falls. The lower falls are actually a series of five small cascades around a midstream island. A pathway from the nearby campground follows the river to a viewing platform overlooking a portion of the falls. To view the remainder of the cascades, rent a rowboat from the park concession and row to the island.

From the lower falls, the Tahquamenon River continues its 94-mile course along the southern edge of the state park to Whitefish Bay. Highway M123 takes a more northerly course through the remainder of Tahquamenon Falls State Park and a portion of the Lake Superior State Forest. Along Highway M123, watch for one of Michigan's newest reintroduced animals, the moose.

Standing up to 7 feet tall at the shoulder and weighing over 1,000 pounds, the moose is the world's largest deer. Yet it blends surprisingly well into its surrounding and is often difficult to spot. The moose favors thickets of aspen, willow, and spruce, where it browses on buds and leaves, and wetlands, where it feeds on aquatic vegetation. If you are lucky enough to spot a moose along the road, maintain a respectful distance. The ungainly and harmless-looking moose is actually quick, agile, and unpredictable. Moose are capable of fearlessly protecting their young, and, when threatened, they have attacked people, automobiles, and even trains.

Highway M123 reaches Whitefish Bay at the aptly named town of Paradise. This town is a popular port of call for fishermen seeking steelhead, salmon, muskellunge, and brown trout in the productive waters of the bay. Paradise is surrounded by some of Michigan's best wild-blueberry habitat. The fire of 1922 destroyed most of the vegetation around Paradise, but also created perfect conditions for wild blueberries. Each August the town celebrates its good fortune by hosting the annual Wild Blueberry Festival, which features pie-eating contests (blueberry, of course), a blueberry brunch, and an arts and crafts fair.

From the town of Paradise, follow Whitefish Point Road north to Whitefish Point. Near the tip of the peninsula, the 80-foot-tall tower of the Whitefish Point Lighthouse has the unfortunate distinction of marking the eastern edge of Lake Superior's "Shipwreck Coast." More vessels have been lost along this stretch of Superior's shoreline than anywhere else on the lake.

When conditions are right, a strong northwest wind has 160 miles of open water in which to churn up huge, destructive waves that can overwhelm even the largest vessel. Storms of great magnitude happen periodically on Lake Superior, but the worst is said to have occurred in 1905, when hurricane-force winds wrecked thirty ships on the lake. Seventy years later, on November 10, 1975, the modern freighter *Edmund Fitzgerald* and its entire crew were lost in a gale as it tried to reach the safety of Whitefish Bay. The night the *Edmund Fitzgerald* sank was the only time in the 126-year history of Whitefish Point Lighthouse that its light malfunctioned.

The Great Lakes Shipwreck Museum occupies the former keeper's dwelling of the Whitefish Point Lighthouse. (The lighthouse was automated in 1970.) The museum was founded in 1986 by a group of scuba divers researching the many perfectly preserved shipwrecks of the Great Lakes. Stories of the men and the ships that were swallowed by the Great Lakes, and exhibits of the rescued artifacts from the tragedies give visitors an appreciation for the peril that sailors face on the five inland seas.

In the frigid waters off Whitefish Point, the 376-square-mile Whitefish Point Underwater Preserve offers hearty scuba divers the chance to visit eighteen shipwrecks at their final resting places. Many of the wrecks are in relatively shallow water, and all are well preserved by Superior's cold temperatures. All artifacts associated with the wrecks are protected by law to ensure each site remains as it was when the vessel was lost. Whitefish Point Underwater Preserve is part of Michigan's underwater-preserve system, which includes nine other sites in the Great Lakes.

Whitefish Point not only guides Great Lakes sailors into safe harbor, but it also serves as a beacon and staging area for migrating birds. Whitefish Point is the last land mass for birds heading north across Lake Superior in the spring, and it is the first land mass reached by those birds migrating south across the lake in the autumn. The Whitefish Point Bird Observatory provides both the scientific community and the "birding" public a place to witness large-scale migration events. Eagles, hawks, falcons, owls, waterfowl, and songbirds pass by or stop to feed at the sanctuary on their way to Canada each spring. In late autumn, the returning birds and their offspring pass by on their way south. A series of boardwalks extending out into the preserve and an information station help visitors get the best views possible of the semiannual spectacle.

The centerpiece of Tahquamenon Falls State Park is Upper Tahquamenon Falls. A short walk along a paved, handicap-accessible path leads to several viewing platforms overlooking the cascade.

FACING PAGE, CLOCKWISE FROM THE TOP:
Autumn brings a riot of color to the low hills and wetlands of the eastern Upper Peninsula.

The shores of Lake Huron in the Les Cheneaux Island region are home to many rare and unusual plants such as Houghton's Goldenrod.

Fireweed blossoms along the roadsides and in open areas throughout the Upper Peninsula.

Highway M134:
Les Cheneaux Islands and Drummond Island

ROUTE 8

From Interstate 75 north of St. Ignace, follow State Highway M134 east to De Tour Village. In downtown De Tour, take the Drummond Island ferry across the De Tour Passage to Drummond Island. Highway M134 continues on Drummond Island. Follow Canoe Bay Road north toward Maxton to the Maxton Plains.

The thirty-six islands known collectively as Les Cheneaux lie off the northern shore of Lake Huron. In Les Cheneaux, proudly noted by its residents as a forgotten corner of Michigan, the slow-paced rhythm of the nineteenth century remains the cadence of daily life. Few other places in Michigan are in step with life on the waters of the Great Lakes the way this region is. In fact, road travel is a fairly recent phenomenon for the small towns along Lake Huron's upper coast. Prior to the 1940s, the only access to this region was by boat.

The Les Cheneaux Islands have provided sailors with shelter from Lake Huron's gales for centuries. The sky blue waters of the archipelago may even hold one of the Great Lakes' most elusive secrets, the fate of the *Griffin*. Built in 1679 on the Upper Niagara River by French explorer René-Robert Cavelier, Sieur de La Salle, the *Griffin* was the first European sailing vessel known to ply the Great Lakes. The ship left for Green Bay on Lake Michigan in the spring of 1679, picked up a cargo of furs valued at over 50,000 francs (about $10,000), and left for a return trip to Niagara in late September. The *Griffin* and her crew were never seen again.

Much conjecture surrounds the events leading to the loss of the *Griffin*. Many blamed the Ottawa or fur traders, accusing them of boarding and burning the ship as it sailed near the shore. Some even accused Jesuits of treachery in destroying the ship. Many others believed that the ship sought shelter from a Lake Huron tempest among the Les Cheneaux Islands and was wrecked on a reef. The argument that the ship sank near Les Cheneaux is convincing enough that the search for the remains of the *Griffin* continues to this day.

During the late nineteenth century, Les Cheneaux Islands drew wealthy tourists with a taste for vacationing in style in a wild and beautiful setting. Eight luxury hotels, with amenities rivaling those at the Grand Hotel on Mackinac Island, sprang up to serve the vacationing steamship and yacht crowd. Many wealthy families built summer homes and cottages in Les Cheneaux that have remained family retreats to this day.

Commercial and sport fishing enjoy a special place in historical and modern times in the Les Cheneaux region. Beginning in 1870, the Hamel family dominated the fishing industry in the region for over a hundred years, hauling in catches of whitefish and lake trout for the commercial market. Today, private vessels and charters ply the cold water of Lake Huron for yellow perch, northern pike, smallmouth bass, and salmon.

With the development of the motorboat in the early twentieth century, the wooden Chris Craft Runabout became the preferred craft for travel among the islands of Les Cheneaux. The handcrafted runabouts were made in Algonac, Michigan, and were sold in Hessel by Eugene Mertaugh, the owner of E. J. Mertaugh Boat Works. To deliver the runabouts to waiting customers, Mertaugh traveled to Algonac and personally drove the small boats through 250 miles of open, storm-prone Lake Huron water back to his boat works in Hessel. Modern-day owners of these beautiful wooden boats gather each August in Hessel for the Antique Wooden Boat Show.

State Highway M134 between Hessel and De Tour Village hugs the shoreline of Lake Huron. The boulder-strewn shore along this portion of Lake Huron is broken up by the occasional sandy swimming beach, and much of it is protected as a permanent natural area. The Nature Conservancy, a conservation group that purchases at-risk natural areas to protect them from development, has acquired over 8 miles of shoreline along the route. Watch for a pull-off just east of Cedarville, where a sign explains the Nature Conservancy's mission in the region and a nature trail meanders through a cedar forest along the protected shoreline.

From De Tour Village you can drive your vehicle onto the Drummond Island ferry for a short ride across De Tour Passage to Drummond Island. The narrow passage where the St. Mary's River meets Lake Huron is one of the busiest shipping channels on the Great Lakes. All freighters bound for Lake Superior pass through De Tour Channel, as do vessels headed from Superior to the southern Great Lakes and beyond. Freighter watching is a favorite pastime on De Tour Passage, and the car ferry offers a front-row seat.

Drummond Island consists of 87,000 acres of hardwood forests, cedar swamps, meadows, and exposed limestone bedrock, all sandwiched within 150 miles of sand and rock beach. Two-thirds of the island is state-owned and open to all forms of outdoor recreation. History buffs can visit the Drummond Island Historical Museum for a look at native artifacts and relics from Fort Drummond, the last British military outpost on American soil.

One particularly interesting area on Drummond Island is the Maxton Plains, located on the northern portion of the island, off Maxton Road. The treeless, 400-million-year-old, exposed limestone bedrock of the plains is known as an alvar, a unique geological feature found only in portions of Canada, the United States, and Sweden. The Maxton Plains is the largest, high-quality alvar left in North America. The seemingly barren landscape of weathered limestone is home to ten of Michigan's rarest plants; both arctic and prairie species grow in the thin soil and in the cracks of the bedrock. A large portion of the plains is state land, and an additional 2,017 acres are owned by the Nature Conservancy.

Drummond Island and the archipelago dotting its shores mark the northwestern edge of Lake Huron's famous North Channel. From Drummond Island south to Ontario's Georgia Bay, boaters enjoy the protection and beauty of a string of large and small islands along Lake Huron's northeast coast. The North Channel has been a favorite passage from lower Lake Huron to the St. Mary's River since the days of the fur trade.

PART II

WHERE THE NORTH BEGINS:
THE UPPER LOWER PENINSULA

FACING PAGE:
Wild iris (Iris versicolor) blossom in a wetlands.

ABOVE:
Fishing boats ply the waters around Manistee's lighthouse, hoping to catch salmon as they head into the Manistee River to spawn.

To many Michiganders, up north begins when you cross Highway M55 and the farmland of central Michigan turns into forests of pine and hardwoods. This is the land of quiet lakes and forests where icy rivers teem with trout. This is also Lower Michigan's Snow Belt, where 70 to 150 inches of snow falls annually. Snowmobiling and skiing draw nearly as many visitors to the area each winter as do family vacations in the summer months.

Large tracts of public land can be found throughout the upper Lower Peninsula. The Huron-Manistee National Forest, several large state forests, and many state parks provide thousands of acres of outdoor recreation land to explore and enjoy. The forests of the lower Upper Peninsula harbor an amazing variety of animals and birds. White-tailed deer, elk, black bear, porcupine, ruffed grouse, bald eagle, and hundreds of other species thrive here. World-class trout streams and hundreds of lakes draw fishermen from around the country.

Interstate 75 runs north/south through the middle of the upper Lower Peninsula, providing quick access to two of our backroads destinations. A short drive from Interstate 75 on a well-maintained road will take you to the other routes in this section. There is much to see and do in this area of Michigan, so if an attraction intrigues you, be sure to follow your curiosity.

TIP OF THE MITT:
MACKINAC TO WILDERNESS STATE PARK

ROUTE 9

From Interstate 75 at Mackinaw City, follow Business Route 75 into the city. Downtown is east of the Mackinac Bridge, and Colonial Michilimackinac is to the west. To visit the Mill Creek area, follow U.S. Highway 23 south toward Cheboygan.

To reach Wilderness State Park from Mackinaw City, take westbound Central Avenue to Meadowlands Road and turn south. At Trails End Road, turn on Wilderness Park Drive. Follow the signs to Wilderness State Park. To reach the southern side of Wilderness State Park, follow C81 south to Lakeview Road and head west.

Mention "the Straits," "the Bridge," or fudge to anyone who has vacationed in northern Michigan, and they will know that you mean the Mackinac (pronounced MACK-in-AWE) area at the tip of Michigan's lower peninsula. Mackinaw City and Mackinac Island are two of the state's premier vacation destinations, and the Mackinac Bridge delivers thousands of visitors each year to Michigan's Upper Peninsula. Today, tourists from around the world come to enjoy scenery, shopping, boating, fishing, and first-class lodging at the tip of the mitten, and hardly anyone who visits Mackinaw City or Mackinac Island leaves without sampling a piece of Mackinac fudge.

The tip of Michigan's mitten has been a focal point for human activity for as long as people have traveled the Great Lakes. The Ottawa, Chippewa, and Huron peoples camped here in the summer, filling their canoes with whitefish and lake trout and boiling maple syrup in birchbark kettles. Jesuit missionaries passed through on their way to the unexplored interior of North America, and the French, British, and Americans fought to control the strategic waters of the Straits of Mackinac.

Just west of modern-day Mackinaw City, the cedar pickets of Colonial Michilimackinac stand at the water's edge on Lake Michigan. From about 1715, when the French built Fort Michilimackinac, until 1781, when the British abandoned this same fort for safer ground on Mackinac Island, Fort Michilimackinac was the seat of European military power in the Upper Great Lakes. Under the French, Fort Michilimackinac was more of a fortified trading post than a base for military operations. The outpost provided

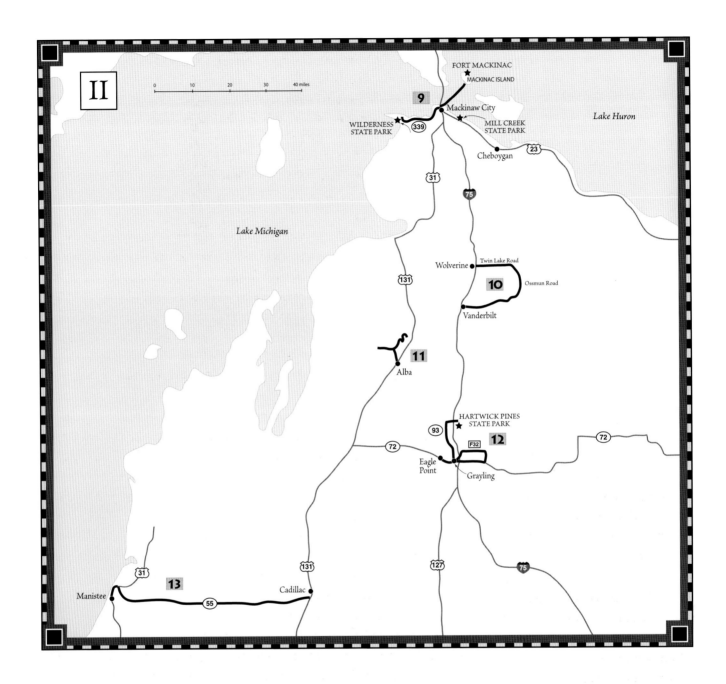

Colonial Michilimackinac is an authentically reconstructed fort and trading post originally built in 1715 to house French soldiers and fur traders. The fort was later occupied by the British military after the French ceded much of their New World holdings to Britain following the French and Indian War.

Costumed interpreters re-enact life at Colonial Michilimackinac during the mid-1700s.

The five-mile-long Mackinac Bridge spans the Straights of Mackinac between Michigan's Upper and Lower Peninsulas.

French traders and their Native American allies with supplies, as the French traded European utensils and weapons for furs from the western Great Lakes area and Canada.

When France ceded its New World territories to the British after the French and Indian War, a contingent of British redcoats took control of Fort Michilimackinac. The French laissez-faire attitude and good treatment of their Native American trading partners was not extended by the new British administrators, however, and resentment soon turned to violence.

On June 2, 1763, at the height of Pontiac's Rebellion against the British, a group of 350 Chippewa arrived at Fort Michilimackinac and organized a game of lacrosse outside the walls of the stockade. Unbeknownst to the British soldiers who had come outside the fort to watch, the game of lacrosse was a clever diversion. When the ball was "accidentally" tossed over the garrison wall, the Chippewa warriors rushed inside, catching the British completely by surprise. In a matter of minutes, the whole contingent of British soldiers was either killed or captured.

One of the few British citizens to escape harm that day was Alexander Henry, an adventurer and trader whose life was saved by a Chippewa family he had befriended. Henry later became a key figure in the fur trade and

The Mackinac Bridge opened in 1957 with a parade of brand-new automobiles. The bridge celebrated its 100 millionth crossing in 1998. Courtesy of State of Michigan Archives/negative #18145

in the exploration of Michigan, and he wrote of his many adventures living among the Native Americans of the Great Lakes.

Today, the reconstructed fort is called Colonial Michilimackinac. A visit to Colonial Michilimackinac features a guided walking tour of the fort, musket and cannon firings, pioneer-skills demonstrations, native crafts, and a museum of artifacts from the site. The ongoing excavation at Michilimackinac is the longest continuous archeological dig in the nation.

Mackinaw City is a town built around tourism. On a summer's afternoon, the large downtown bustles with visitors strolling through galleries, gift shops, clothing stores, restaurants, bookstores, arcades, and fudge shops. Along the waterfront, pleasure craft of every description line the slips of the public dock. A waterfront park on the north side of town is a nice place to watch 600-foot-long lake freighters slip under the Mackinac Bridge like bathtub toys. Historic churches, well-kept Victorian homes, museums, and parks make Mackinaw City one of Michigan's most popular destinations.

South of Mackinaw City on U.S. Highway 23 is Historic Mill Creek, a reconstructed, water-powered sawmill. Built by Scotsman Robert Campbell in the 1780s, the Mill Creek sawmill was one of the first industrial sites in the Great Lakes. The 625-acre site contains a millwright's house, where craftsmen are using period tools to reconstruct a home and a blacksmith shop. Historic Mill Creek also features costumed interpreters, a working sawmill demonstration, and 3.5 miles of nature trails.

No trip to the Mackinac area would be complete without a trip to Mackinac Island. Accessible only by boat (or snowmobile in the winter), travel on the island is limited to horse-drawn carriage, bicycle, or foot. The historic downtown district is a collection of beautifully maintained eighteenth- and nineteenth-century buildings, where costumed interpreters tell the story of each building and its former occupants. The island also has a butterfly farm, miles of walking and biking trails, and Fort Mackinac, a fully restored Revolutionary War–era fort.

Built in 1887, the Grand Hotel on Mackinac Island is Michigan's premier resort hotel. Shirts and ties are the norm at this hotel, even when lounging on the hotel's 660-foot-long, pillared front porch. (Luncheon guests are welcome without formal attire.) The classic Greek design of the hotel's exterior is as unusual today as it was when the hotel was first built among the Victorian cottages on the island. The Grand has managed to maintain its nineteenth-century formal style through the years while keeping pace with modern hotel practices and amenities. The hotel has been the setting for movies, including *This Time for Keeps* with Jimmy Durante and Esther Williams and *Somewhere in Time*, starring Christopher Reeves and Jane Seymour. It has also hosted dozens of political and business conventions.

At their first meeting in 1888, the board of directors of the newly opened Grand Hotel on Mackinac Island called for a bridge to be built across the straits to complement their new hotel. For the next century, many ideas for a link between the peninsulas were put forward, including a floating tun-

FACING PAGE. CLOCKWISE FROM THE TOP:
Built in 1892, the Old Mackinac Point Lighthouse has recently been restored and is open for tours.

The preferred mode of transportation on Mackinac Island is the bicycle.

Historic Mill Creek features a water-powered sawmill rebuilt at the site of the first sawmill on the Straights of Mackinac. The original mill provided lumber for buildings on Mackinac Island in the late eighteenth and early nineteenth centuries.

THIS PAGE, CLOCKWISE FROM THE TOP:
Beautiful Victorian homes line the residential streets on Mackinac Island.

Fine detail and fanciful design are the hallmark of many of the houses and buildings on Mackinac Island.

Mackinac Island's many bed-and-breakfast establishments offer a variety of places to kick back and relax.

nel and a series of causeways between the islands in the straits. In 1934, the Mackinac Bridge Authority was created to study the feasibility of a bridge, and nineteen years later, work was officially begun on the Mackinac Bridge. The first traffic crossed the straits on "Big Mac" on November 1, 1957.

A masterpiece of modern engineering, the 5-mile-long Mackinac Bridge connects Michigan's Upper and Lower peninsulas. The main towers of the suspension bridge stand 552 feet above the water and extend another 210 feet below the water's surface. Two-foot-diameter steel cables, each containing 12,580 individual wire cables, support the suspension bridge; 4,851,700 steel rivets and over 1 million steel bolts hold everything together. To erect the bridge, 3,500 workers were employed at the bridge site, and another 7,500 worked at the shops, quarries, and mills that produced the building materials.

Hardwood forests, dense stands of conifers, wet meadows dotted with ponds, and 26 miles of sandy Lake Michigan shoreline make Wilderness State Park an important refuge for animals, endangered birds, rare plants, and nature-loving people. A network of hiking, mountain-biking, and cross-country-skiing trails crisscross the park's 8,286 acres, passing through the haunts of black bear, white-tailed deer, snowshoe hare, mink, otter, porcupine, and coyote. The wet meadows are home to some of Michigan's rarest orchids, and the secluded beaches on Lake Michigan are the nesting ground for the endangered piping plover.

With its sweeping view of the Straits of Mackinac, the 627-foot-long veranda of the Grand Hotel on Mackinac Island is still a popular place for lunch, dinner, or relaxation. Courtesy of State of Michigan Archives/negative # 00887

Two campgrounds offer a total of 250 modern campsites for visitors to enjoy, along with six rustic backcountry cabins and three bunkhouses. Wilderness camping is also allowed along the park's trails. The park receives a lot of hunting pressure during the autumn and winter months, so be sure to wear bright clothing when hiking during that time of the year. A large metal-detecting area has also been set aside within the park to accommodate hobbyists. The southern portion of the park contains only hiking trails and undeveloped Lake Michigan shoreline, making it a great spot to escape the crowds and enjoy a walk through undisturbed Michigan forest.

PIGEON RIVER COUNTRY STATE FOREST

Sprawling and untamed, remote yet accessible, Pigeon River Country State Forest offers 98,000 acres of quintessential northern Lower Peninsula landscape. Gentle hills crowned with maple, beech, and pine enclose valleys and meadows that echo with the autumn bugle of bull elk. The Black, Sturgeon, and Pigeon rivers flow clear and swift through the state forest, providing near-perfect habitat for brook, brown, and rainbow trout. Pigeon River Country is wild enough to accommodate loons, elk, black bears, and bald eagles, yet accessible to everyone from family campers to backpackers.

Pigeon River Country was assured a special place in the hearts of Michigan's outdoor enthusiasts in 1918, when two-dozen Rocky Mountain elk were released in the state forest. Elk were once plentiful in Michigan, but deforestation and hunting during the nineteenth century drove them to extinction. The reintroduction of the Rocky Mountain elk has proven a huge success, and the current herd is the largest east of the Mississippi River. A strictly regulated hunting season opens each fall, but elk watching remains a far more popular activity. Check at the forest headquarters for up-to-date information on the best places to view elk.

A portion of Pigeon River Country State Forest has been set aside as a "no-motorized-vehicle area" for those who wish to enjoy the scenery as well as the quiet of the forest. Known as the Green Timbers Recreation Area, the trails of this 6,300-acre parcel on the forest's western edge are popular with mountain bikers, cross-country skiers, and hikers. The remainder of the state forest is open to snowmobiles and receives heavy use during the winter.

There are seven state forest campgrounds within Pigeon River Country. They feature only the basic necessities: pit toilets, a water pump, picnic tables, and a fire ring. The campgrounds at Pigeon Bridge and at the Pigeon River are great places to fish for trout. In fact, a 30-mile portion of the upper Pigeon is designated as a Michigan Blue Ribbon Trout Stream (BRTS). The thirty-nine-site campground on the shores of Pickerel Lake offers great bass, panfish, and rainbow-trout fishing.

A love for the special character of Pigeon River Country has inspired many people to dedicate themselves to its well-being. To P. S. Lovejoy, noted preservationist and director of the Michigan Department of Conservation in the early twentieth century, Pigeon River Country was the "Big Wild." Under

ROUTE 10

From the Vanderbilt exit on Interstate 75, turn east into town and then turn north (left) on Main Street. Main Street will turn into Sturgeon Valley Road outside of town. Follow Sturgeon Valley Road to Twin Lake Road and turn north. Pigeon River Country State Forest headquarters is located on Twin Lake Road. At the headquarters you will find maps of the state forest, elk-watching information, and other general information about the area.

Well-marked trails lead hikers into the interior of the Pigeon River Country State Forest. In winter the trails become cross-country ski runs.

The Fragrant Water Lily is a common aquatic flower in the Pigeon River Country State Forest.

The Pigeon River is one of several Blue Ribbon Trout Streams that flow through the Pigeon River Country State Forest.

The drive-in campgrounds found in Pigeon River Country State Forest are quiet and well maintained. Most are located on the shores of small lakes or along scenic stretches of river.

Lovejoy, the Michigan Department of Conservation replanted forestland in Pigeon River Country that had been laid to waste by years of clear-cut logging and forest fires. More importantly, Lovejoy changed the attitude people held toward public forestlands. He viewed Michigan's forests as a natural resource that should be carefully managed, not as a source of quick income for the timber industry.

In the 1970s, oil drilling was proposed in Pigeon River Country. Conservation groups, sportsmen groups, and individual citizens threw their support behind the Department of Natural Resources in a battle with Michigan Oil Company. The right of Michigan's government to regulate the use of public land was finally decided by the Michigan Supreme Court in favor of the conservation community and the Department of Natural Resources. A compromise was reached that allowed limited and regulated drilling in Pigeon River Country as long as steps were taken to prevent pollution and the aesthetics of the forest were maintained. Today's threat to Pigeon River Country comes from development pressure, habitat fragmentation, and overuse. Still, with all the pressures on the region, Pigeon River Country remains one of the premier wilderness areas in the Lower Peninsula.

WHAT IS A TWO-TRACK?

As you follow the maintained roads through Pigeon River Country State Forest or other state land in northern Michigan, you will see unimproved "two-track" roads leading off the main thoroughfares. As the name implies, a two-track is simply two tire tracks, usually with grass growing in between, that have been used in the past as a fire road or a logging access road. Some two-tracks lead to lakes or streams, others lead to secluded hunting or berry-picking sites, and some simply lead to a dead end. Wherever they lead, "two-tracking" in a vehicle, on a mountain bike, or on foot can be a great way to spot wildlife and see the countryside.

Most two-tracks are not marked in any official sense, and many do not appear on any map. Sometimes you may find a handmade sign nailed to a tree to guide travelers to someone's cabin or property, but usually there are no road signs whatsoever. Two-tracks rarely follow a straight course and are usually crisscrossed by other two-tracks. As you can imagine, it is easy to get lost in a maze of roads that all look similar and all twist around the points of the compass. Despite the obvious danger of getting lost, two-tracking can be a lot of fun if basic precautions are taken.

To avoid a long walk, fill up the gas tank before you begin. A GPS unit or a compass and a map showing the main roads of the area will prove handy if you happen to become turned around. A shovel can save the day if you get stuck in a sand trap. A bow saw will make life easy if you have to clear a fallen tree from the roadway, and extra water and food are always a good idea.

You can prevent a lot of problems by keeping your eyes open for hazards and by using common sense when driving on a two-track. Drive slowly and watch for loose sand or potholes full of water in the road; check out these hazards before driving through them. Stay on the road, and if you need to turn around, do so at a crossroad or at a spot that has been cleared of vegetation. Also, be aware that your muffler and catalytic converter are hot enough to start a grass fire, and never park over a patch of dry grass. Most importantly, enjoy your travels along Michigan's uncharted two-tracks, and keep them intact for the next adventurous traveler.

JORDAN RIVER VALLEY

The pure waters, biological integrity, and beautifully forested watershed of the Jordan River made it a natural choice to receive Michigan's first Wild and Scenic River designation in 1972. Shallow and clear, the Jordan rises from the wooded moraines and glacial plains of the Jordan River State Forest. A valley of red maple, white ash, yellow birch, basswood, and beech surround the river, and spruce, tamarack, and cedar line its bank. The Jordan's narrow course is strewn with fallen trees and logs—perfect hideouts for the native brook trout and stocked brown trout that fill its pure waters.

The Jordan River valley lies near the headwaters of the Jordan River in northwestern Antrim County. From the village of Gaylord, take State Highway M32 west to U.S. Highway 131 (about 12 miles), head south on U.S. 131 to Deadman Hill Road, and turn west. Follow the signs to the Deadman Hill Overlook parking area. A logging accident gave Deadman Hill its rather macabre name. In 1902, a logging wheel (a set of huge metal wheels beneath which a log was slung) broke free and tumbled down the hill, killing an unfortunate logger.

Despite its name, the view from Deadman Hill is anything but gloomy. The silver thread of the Jordan River glimmers through a sea of trees as it winds westward toward its outlet at Lake Charlevoix. In the summer, the valley below the overlook is a patchwork of greens. From mid- to late October, the cool green of the cedar and spruce trees intermingle with the brazen colors of the hardwoods, creating one of Michigan's best autumn scenic overlooks.

The summit of Deadman Hill is also the trailhead for the 18-mile-long Jordan River Pathway, a hiking trail through the heart of the Jordan River valley. A large portion of the trail follows the grade of an old railroad, built by the East Jordan Lumber Company in 1918. The early 1900s saw extensive logging activity in the valley, but by 1925, the mills, camps, and lumberjacks were gone and the land began to heal. Today, a hike down the trail leads through a rejuvenated landscape full of beauty and life.

For a drive through the Jordan River valley, return to U.S. 131 and head north 1 mile to Jordan River Road. The gravel road roughly follows the course of the Jordan River through the valley for 15 miles, crossing the river four times. Of all Michigan's backroad routes, the trip though the Jordan River valley is the most adventurous. The hard-packed, sand-and-gravel road is seldom traveled and only sporadically maintained; it may be rutted or may hold standing water in the spring or after a heavy rain. Jordan River Road supports two-way traffic, but it is often wide enough for only one vehicle at a time. If an opposing vehicle presents itself, pull to the right and signal the other driver on, or proceed slowly if the other vehicle pulls off.

Springtime is the season of wildflowers along the Jordan River. Trilliums, orchids, and wild irises bring much-welcomed color to the open woods and the riverbank. Basket-toting hunters can be found prowling the woodlands

ROUTE 11

From U.S. Highway 131 and State Highway M32 East, travel south approximately 0.5 mile to Jordan River Road and turn west. Follow Jordan River Road through the valley to the junction with Pinney Bridge Road. To exit the valley and return to U.S. 131, follow Jordan River Road to the left. To continue through the valley to Graves Crossing and the state forest campground, follow Pinney Bridge Road to the right. Exit the valley at State Highway M66, off Pinney Bridge Road. To view Deadman Hill, follow U.S. 131 south from Highway M32, east to Deadman Hill Road, and turn west. Follow the signs to Deadman Hill Overlook.

FACING PAGE:
Wild iris grows along the banks of the Jordan River.

LEFT:
Jordan River Road passes through the heart of the Jordan Valley.

BOTTOM LEFT:
The Jordan River Valley is home to an amazing array of plants and animals. This colorful mushroom is a poisonous member of the Russula family.

BOTTOM RIGHT:
Many types of orchid, such as this showy lady's slipper, are native to the Jordan River Valley.

for Michigan's springtime delicacy: the wild morel mushroom. The opening of trout season in April brings fishermen hoping to lure a trophy from one of the river's riffles, runs, pools, or logjams. The Jordan does not easily give up its resident trout. Fly-fishermen find the narrow, tree-lined, snag-filled river an easier place to tangle their line than to land a fish.

A summer drive along Jordan River Road passes through sunny meadows and into the twilight of the mature forest. In the morning and evening, watch for the always-alert white-tailed deer browsing on meadow grasses at the forest's edge. Wild turkey, beaver, otter, mink, ruffed grouse, and woodcock also call the varied habitats of the valley home. The roadway is also a great place to observe many different species of butterflies as they mud in damp areas of the road. Several small parking areas along the route provide river access for a summer's day of fishing in the solitude of the Jordan wilderness.

Jordan River Road provides a chance for an up-close look at the symphony of fall color spread out below the overlook at Deadman Hill. By mid-October, a majority of the hardwood trees are wearing their best autumn colors, and, soon after, red, yellow, orange, and brown leaves carpet the ground. In the meadows, small groves of aspen and solitary maple and chokecherry trees glow against the backdrop of the fading yellow grasses. Autumn rains bring a colorful variety of mushrooms to life, from the subtle chestnut rings of the turkey tail to the bold yellow and orange amanita (a toxic mushroom sometimes called the "Death Cap").

Winter brings snowmobilers and snowshoers to the Jordan River valley. The valley lies in Lower Michigan's snowbelt, which receives an average of nearly 100 inches of snow each season. When the snow starts flying in late November, the East Jordan Snowmobile Club lays out trails along the Jordan and often hosts snowmobile safaris through the river's pristine winter watershed. Jordan River Road is not plowed in the winter, so backcountry access for snowshoeing is limited to Deadman Hill or the Pinney Bridge area.

The fisheries of Lakes Michigan and Huron provide jobs and recreation for residents of all the Great Lakes states as well as Ontario, Canada. To keep the lake trout population at high levels, the Jordan River National Fish Hatchery supplies 1.8 million lake trout annually to stock in Lake Huron and Lake Michigan. At any given time, the hatchery may have between 2 million and 5 million lake-trout fingerlings at various stages of growth. Over fourteen thousand people tour the hatchery each year; its visitor center is open year-round. The hatchery is accessible either from Jordan River Road or from Turner Road, west of U.S. 131.

A short distance past the hatchery, Jordan River Road splits off to the left and climbs out of the valley to the small town of Alba and U.S. 131. Pinney Bridge Road continues through the valley to Graves Crossing State Forest Campground and to State Highway M66.

Big Trout and Big Trees:
Grayling and the AuSable River

More often than not, location is everything. Take the city of Grayling, for instance. It is located in Crawford County, where only 1 mile separates the AuSable River, which flows east into Lake Huron, and the Manistee River, which flows west toward Lake Michigan. For Native Americans and French traders, this feature made the area a natural hub for moving goods and people from one coast of Michigan to the other. When Grayling's white-pine forests fell under the saw during the logging boom of the late 1800s, the logging companies were able to float their product to market down the nearby AuSable River. Grayling's luck held in the 1960s when Interstate 75 was built through the city, opening a new route for local manufacturers to move their goods to markets around the country.

Although Grayling has always provided its residents and visitors with opportunities in a setting of great natural beauty, it seems that it was not easy to find an appropriate name for the town. At various times the community has been called AuSable, Forest, Crawford Station, and Milltown. The area's first settler, Michael Hartwick, built a log hotel in 1872. One year later, the Jackson, Lansing, and Saginaw Railroad Company platted out 40 acres of land around Hartwick's hotel and named the settlement Crawford. The name Crawford lasted until1874, when Ruben Babbit took to Daniel Fitzhue in Bay City several fish he had caught, but could not identify, from the AuSable River. The identity of the fish, with their streamlined, troutlike bodies and enormous dorsal fins, stumped Fitzhue, too, so Babbit sent the specimens on to Washington, D.C. When Babbit and his fellow townspeople found out that the mystery fish were called grayling, they decided that Grayling sounded better than Crawford and thus renamed the town.

It was logging that turned Grayling from an isolated outpost of the 1860s to a bustling town of 2,500 people by the end of the nineteenth century. Artifacts and memorabilia from the days when Grayling was a major center of commerce in northern Michigan are displayed at the Crawford County Historical Museum on Michigan Avenue in downtown Grayling. The museum is housed in a restored railroad depot, and features exhibits and photographs depicting life in Grayling in the late nineteenth and early twentieth centuries. On the museum grounds you can visit a railroad caboose, a trapper's cabin, an antique farm building, and an old firehouse.

A big part of Grayling's identity comes from nearby Camp Grayling, a Michigan National Guard base south and west of town. Founded in 1913, the base covers 147,000 acres in Kalkaska, Crawford, and Otsego counties. Each year the camp schedules training for over twenty thousand military personnel, including National Guard and regular army units. When train-

Route 12

From Business Route 75 in Grayling, follow South Down River Road (State Highway M72) east toward Mio. At Stephen's Bridge Road, turn north. Stephen's Bridge crosses the main branch of the AuSable River. At North Down River Road, turn west back toward Grayling. At Business Route 75, turn north (right) and follow State Highway M93 to Hartwick Pines State Park, or turn left toward town and pick up Highway M72 west to visit Lake Margrethe.

RIGHT:

A set of logging wheels sits at the entrance to Hartwick Pines State Park. The eight foot tall wheels were used to haul cut logs.

BELOW:

The Old Growth Forest Foot Trail in Hartwick Pines State Park meanders through one of the last remaining old-growth forests in Lower Michigan.

FACING PAGE:

Morning mist rises over Bright Lake in Hartwick Pines State Park. Bright Lake and its neighbor, Glory Lake, were named for a team of oxen that once hauled cut logs out of the forest.

ing is not taking place, most areas of Camp Grayling are open for public recreation, including hunting, fishing, snowmobiling, and cross-country skiing. The base surrounds Lake Margrethe, a favorite stop for fishermen and boaters. A public boat launch at a U.S. Forest Service campground provides access to the lake.

The namesake of Lake Margrethe was Margrethe Hanson, the wife of lumber baron Rasmus Hanson, who donated the original tract of land for Camp Grayling. In 1916 he also founded the Grayling Fish Hatchery Club to help reinforce the natural populations of fish in the AuSable River. Although the original aim of the club was to restore grayling to the river, an endeavor that ultimately failed, the club did manage to keep the river well stocked with brook and brown trout. The hatchery was sold to the state of Michigan in 1926 and continued operation until it was closed in the 1960s. A citizens' committee revived the hatchery and reopened it to the public in 1983. A small entrance fee keeps the facility operating and entitles visitors to view trophy-sized trout up close.

All of Grayling's attributes notwithstanding, it is the beautiful AuSable River that has endeared this small northern town to so many people. The river's cedar-lined banks are seldom more than 100 feet apart, and the cold water runs sparkling clear over a sand-and-gravel bottom. A twisting,

Horse-drawn sleds were used to move logs along specially built ice roads from the lumber camps to the mills. Courtesy of State of Michigan Archives/negative #16112

turning course has undercut the river's banks and has formed deep pools and shallow eddies where brook, brown, and rainbow trout face the current and await their next meal. The AuSable is one of Michigan's premier trout streams, and fly-fishing rules here.

Many areas of the AuSable River downstream of Grayling are the exclusive domain of fly-fishers, and on some stretches of the river, a catch-and-release policy is maintained. Angling in the AuSable requires a Michigan fishing license with a trout stamp.

The best way to experience the AuSable's legendary fishing is to hire a guide with an AuSable riverboat from one of the many outfitters in the area. The shallow wooden riverboats have evolved over the years into the perfect fly-fishing vessel. The guide sits in the rear and maneuvers the boat with a pole, while, up front, the fisherman casts the river from the comfort of a padded chair.

To access the river by car, take South Down River Road (State Highway M72) east from Grayling toward Mio. Turn north on either Burtons Landing Road or Keystone Landing Road; both lead to access points along the river. To cross the AuSable and head back toward town, turn north on Stephens Bridge Road and then west on North Down River Road. From North Down River Road, you can access the river at the AuSable River Canoe Camp.

Canoeing the AuSable or the nearby Manistee River is a great way to spend a summer's afternoon. Grayling is home to several canoe liveries, which offer river trips ranging from a couple of hours in length to daylong excursions. In July, the town hosts the Weyerhaeuser AuSable River Canoe Marathon. Beginning in Grayling on Saturday morning, the contestants paddle through the night to the finish line in Oscoda, 120 miles away on the shores of Lake Huron. Spectators follow the race from start to finish by driving to a series of observation points along the river, cheering the contestants as they pass.

In the days before the whipsaw was put to work to feed a growing country's insatiable hunger for lumber, it is said that a squirrel could pass from tree to tree across the state of Michigan without ever touching the ground. The ancient forests and the men who worked harvesting them are gone, leaving a legacy that has become a part of the collective story of the people of Michigan. That story is retold along the Old Growth Forest Foot Trail, at the Hartwick Pines Logging Museum, and at the Michigan Forest Visitor Center in Hartwick Pines State Park.

At nearly 10,000 acres, Hartwick Pines State Park is the largest state park in the Lower Peninsula. The park began when Karen Michelson Hartwick gave 8,000 acres of land—including 85 acres of virgin, old-growth forest—to the State of Michigan, in memory of her late husband, Major Edward E. Hartwick. Major Hartwick died overseas in World War I, and Mrs. Hartwick, the daughter of a partner in the Salling-Hanson logging company, wished to keep his memory and that of her family's logging heritage alive. Mrs. Hart-

The AuSable River is a world-renowned trout stream, harboring brook, brown, and rainbow trout.

The "Chapel in the Pines" stands on a small hill in the Old Growth Forest in Hartwick Pines State Park. The small chapel is a favorite location for intimate wedding ceremonies.

Winter snow cloaks the cedar and white pine trees of the Old Growth Forest in Hartwick Pines State Park.

Debris left over from logging operations provided kindling for massive forest fires that scorched Michigan's countryside in the aftermath of the logging boom. Courtesy of State of Michigan Archives/ negative #00065

wick requested that a museum, dedicated to the logging history of the area, be built within the park. In 1934 and 1935, the Civilian Conservation Corps erected a loggers' bunkhouse, a mess hall, a camp office, and a store. On the grounds of the museum, the tools of the nineteenth-century logging industry are on display.

The Michigan Forest Visitor Center serves as a gateway to the Old Growth Forest Foot Trail. In the Michigan Forest Visitor Center's 1,500-square-foot exhibit hall are displays and exhibits depicting the origin of Michigan's forests, the lumbering era, forestry products of the past and today, and what the future holds for forest management in Michigan. A fourteen-minute slide presentation in the center's auditorium sums up the story of forest management past and present.

The real treasure that Karen Hartwick deeded to the people of Michigan was the 85 acres of old-growth forest. Unfortunately, a massive windstorm in 1940 destroyed 36 acres of old trees, leaving only 49 acres for future generations to enjoy. Still, to walk among the towering white pines that frame the Old Growth Forest Foot Trail is to be reminded of the slow and steady process that raises forests and mountains, and the need to use our natural resources wisely.

The Civilian Conservation Corps (CCC) was instrumental in restoring Michigan's forests after the logging boom. CCC camps were run in a quasimilitary style and many CCC workers were housed in tents until more comfortable quarters could be built. A museum dedicated to the work of the CCC is located at North Higgins Lake State Park. Courtesy of State of Michigan Archives

MANISTEE NATIONAL FOREST:
M55 FROM CADILLAC TO MANISTEE

In the aftermath of the devastating logging practices of the nineteenth century, and from the ashes of the ensuing forest fires, Michigan's state and national forest system was born. Land that had been stripped of its timber and abandoned, together with thousands of acres of vacated farmland, was snatched up by the state and federal government. To stabilize the damaged landscape, government programs such as the Civilian Conservation Corps oversaw the replanting of tens of millions of trees, the restoration of wetlands and rivers, and the building of dozens of new park facilities. Today, Michigan's state and federal forest system is the largest east of the Mississippi River. The thriving, second-growth public forests of Michigan provide habitat for an abundance of wildlife, watershed protection for lakes and rivers, renewable resources, recreational opportunities, and scenic splendor for citizens and visitors.

Michigan's state forests encompass over 3.8 million acres, stretching across the state on both peninsulas. Add the state's three national forests—the Ottawa, Hiawatha, and Huron-Manistee—at roughly 1 million acres each, and you have a substantial percentage of Michigan's land held in the public domain.

Our route from Cadillac to Manistee follows State Highway M55 as it passes through the heart of the Huron-Manistee National Forest, where open forests of oak, maple, aspen, and pine cover the rolling terrain. Bracken fern grow knee-deep beneath the canopy of branches, providing cover for ruffed grouse and a host of other small animals. In October, when the hardwoods shed their red, yellow, and orange leaves, the frost-burned fronds of the bracken fern collect and display the discarded leaves like Christmas lights.

The lumber town of Cadillac owes its early prosperity to Ephraim Shay, the inventor of the Shay Locomotive. Unlike most timber towns, Cadillac was not located on a river or near the shores of the Great Lakes. Moving cut logs from the forest to the sawmill without the benefit of a waterway was costly and slow, and the railroads of the time could not climb steep grades, maneuver around sharp curves, or run dependably on imperfect tracks. Shay's locomotive could do all these things, and it quickly revolutionized logging and mining in remote or mountainous regions. The Shay Locomotive was manufactured in Cadillac by the Michigan Iron Works and was used throughout the United States until the 1940s. A restored Shay Locomotive is on display at Cadillac's Waterfront Park.

Surrounded by the Pere Marquette State Forest and the Huron-Manistee National Forest, Cadillac is a thriving, year-round outdoor-recreation town. Fishermen ply the waters of Lake Cadillac and nearby Lake Mitchell for

ROUTE 13

From Cadillac, follow State Highway M55 west to Manistee. To visit the Carl T. Johnson Hunting and Fishing Center, follow State Highway M115 a short distance north from the intersection of Highway M55. To access Tippy Dam, follow Tippy Dam Road north from Highway M55, west of Cadillac.

ABOVE:

The architecture in downtown Manistee gave rise to the town's nickname, the "Victorian Port City."

LEFT:

Wildflower gardens, herb gardens, and small arboretums surround the M. E. Gertrude Gray Manor at the Lake Bluff Audubon Center north of Orchard Beach State Park. The center is noted for its giant sequoia tree, which survives Michigan's harsh winters because of Lake Michigan's moderating effect on the local climate.

FACING PAGE:

The multilevel Manistee Riverwalk extends for 1.5 miles along the Manistee River from Manistee Lake to Lake Michigan.

walleye, bass, perch, and pike, while boaters enjoy the freedom afforded by miles of open water. Mitchell State Park, situated along a manmade channel between the two lakes, has a modern campground where boaters can tie-off their vessels right behind their campsites. The park is also home to the Carl T. Johnson Hunting and Fishing Center.

From its humble headwaters in Otsego County to its robust outfall into Manistee Lake, the Manistee River, north of Highway M55, flows clean and strong through the nicest scenery the northern Lower Peninsula has to offer. Fishermen savor the river for its brook-, rainbow-, and brown-trout populations and its steelhead and king-salmon runs. Canoeists and kayakers enjoy the river's gentle twisting currents and undeveloped, forested banks. The river is dammed at several locations, creating large impoundments. The Tippy Dam Impoundment is especially popular with fishermen due to its northern-pike, muskellunge, walleye, and bass populations. Below the dam, spawning salmon fight their way upstream against the swift spillway-current to an expectant host of wading fishermen. As the Manistee River approaches its terminus, it passes through the wetlands and bayous of the Manistee River State Game Area before flowing through the town of Manistee to Lake Michigan.

With courage and perseverance, the historic town of Manistee has weathered the economic and natural disasters that have beset Michigan over the last 150 years. On October 8, 1871, the same day that Chicago burned to the ground, the lumber slashings and dry timber that surrounded Manistee caught fire. With bucket brigades and the town's one fire engine, residents fought the blaze successfully and then returned to their normal Sunday routine. With no long-distance communication, and the horizon cloaked in the smoke of the first fire, the townspeople had no idea that a second fire, whipped by gale-force winds off Lake Michigan, was working its way toward them. When the fire arrived, there was little to do except flee.

In a scene that was replayed that day from Holland to Tawas City, most of the town and the surrounding countryside were reduced to ashes. In a desperate bid to escape, many townspeople boarded the steamer *Messenger*, which was docked on the river. The steamer's attempt to flee into the safety of Manistee Lake was thwarted when the drawbridge crossing the river burst into flame, effectively blocking the escape route. For what must have seemed an eternity, the ship's captain waited until the bridge collapsed and then, with a full head of steam, surged through the burning debris to safety.

Today, the residents of Manistee refer to their town as the Victorian Port City. The well-maintained Victorian-era storefronts along River Street house an eclectic mix of shops and restaurants. The Manistee River Walk, a multilevel walkway along the river, extends 1.5 miles from U.S. Highway 131 to the shore of Lake Michigan. Two drawbridges across the deepwater channel of the Manistee River allow Great Lakes freighters to pass through the city, stopping traffic and giving bystanders an up-close look at the enormous ships.

The schooner JT Wing enters Manistee Harbor under full sail. The JT Wing was the last commercial schooner to sail the Great Lakes. Courtesy of State of Michigan Archives/negative #06699

PART III

THE SUNSET COAST:
WESTERN LOWER MICHIGAN

FACING PAGE:
The fishing pier at Big Portage Lake in the Waterloo Recreation Area glows in the morning light. Michigan's lakes and rivers offer first class fishing for a variety of gamefish.

ABOVE:
Sugar Maple thrives in the sandy, well-drained soil of Western Michigan.

Great Lakes tourism was born on Michigan's sunset coast. Urban dwellers flocked to the beaches of Lake Michigan in the late eighteenth and early twentieth centuries on steamships and passenger rail. In the late twentieth century, the family automobile provided even more tourists the opportunity to visit the Lake Michigan shore. Today, small towns on Lake Michigan often see their populations increase tenfold as vacationers and cottage owners arrive for their annual summer visit. Many communities along the lakeshore that were founded as mill towns during Michigan's lumber boom owe their continued existence to the summer tourist crowd.

From the border with Indiana on the south, to Mackinaw City at the tip of Michigan's mitten, Lake Michigan's shoreline is essentially one long, sandy beach. Nearly every town on Lake Michigan has a public beach: and state, county, and municipal parks dot the shoreline. Lighthouse lovers treasure Lake Michigan for its many unique and historic lighthouses. Great Lakes maritime history is well preserved at local museums all along the coast.

Lake Michigan's fisheries support a huge commercial and sport fishing industry. An aggressive sea lamprey control program and annual restocking has brought the once depleted lake trout population back to life. Introduced salmon now swarm from the lake into rivers all along the coast each spring and fall to spawn. To capitalize on this abundance of game fish, charter fishing boat services have opened in every town along the lake.

The eastern shore of Lake Michigan contains the largest fresh water dune system on earth. Hills of sand stretch inland from Lake Michigan's beaches, starting as bare piles of sand near the water's edge and finally, through succession, become tree-covered sand hills farther inland. Nearly one half of the 275,000 acres of dunes in Michigan are held in the public domain and are open to be explored and enjoyed.

LITTLE TRAVERSE BAY:
PETOSKEY TO CROSS VILLAGE

ROUTE 14

From Petoskey, follow U.S. Highway 31/U.S. Highway 131 north toward Bay View. Just north of Bay View, follow U.S. 131 north when it splits off toward Harbor Springs. In Harbor Springs, U.S. 131 turns into State Highway M119 and heads north toward the Tunnel of Trees and Cross Village. For a faster return to Harbor Springs, follow County Road 77 south from Cross Village back to Harbor Springs.

From the days of steamship and rail travel to the age of the automobile, Little Traverse Bay has been the destination of choice for people seeking a beautiful, quaint, and friendly place to visit. Through the years the area has seen loggers, mills, and other heavy industry come and go, but Little Traverse Bay has remained a place where urban dwellers seek refuge from the summer heat and stress of the city. Just as in the late nineteenth century, Bay View's immaculate Victorian homes still sit under a canopy of maple trees, Petoskey's Gaslight District still bustles with shoppers, and tourists and locals alike still turn out to watch the sun set over Little Traverse Bay.

One of the twentieth century's greatest writers, Ernest Hemingway, was profoundly influenced by the lifestyle of Little Traverse Bay. Hemingway spent most of his youthful summers kicking around Petoskey and its neighboring towns, taking in the local culture and exploring the woods and waters around the bay. Many of Hemingway's favorite haunts, and many of the people he met during his time in northern Michigan, would later appear as places and

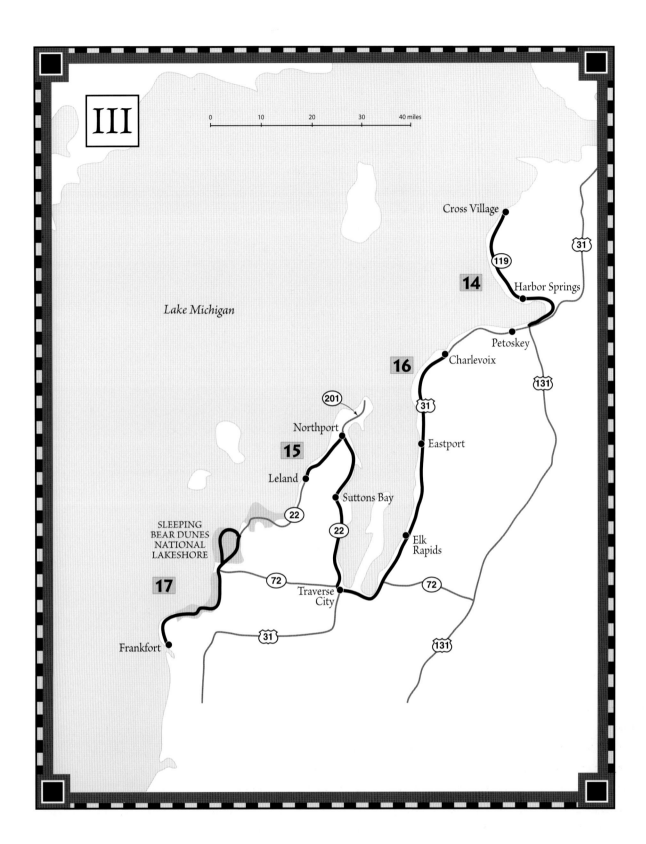

III

0   10   20   30   40 miles

Lake Michigan

Cross Village

119

31

14

Harbor Springs

Petoskey

16

Charlevoix

201

31

Northport

15

Eastport

Leland

Suttons Bay

22

22

131

SLEEPING
BEAR DUNES
NATIONAL
LAKESHORE

Elk
Rapids

17

72

Traverse
City

72

131

31

Frankfort

RIGHT:
Petoskey's Waterfront Park is an excellent place to witness one of Lake Michigan's trademark sunsets.

BELOW:
Legs Inn in Cross Village has been popular a tourist destination since the late 1920s.

The development at Bay Harbor caters to the upscale vacation crowd with luxury accommodations and trendy shops and restaurants.

characters in his short stories. To keep "Papa's" Michigan connection alive, the Michigan Hemingway Society hosts an annual Hemingway Society Fall Weekend each October in Petoskey.

The south side of Little Traverse Bay is dominated by the village of Petoskey and its neighbor to the west, the posh development at Bay Harbor. With a large shopping district (the famous Gaslight District), nearby Petoskey State Park, and several waterfront parks designed for long evening strolls and watching the sun set, Petoskey is a town geared for tourists. The main thoroughfare in Petoskey, U.S. Highway 31, is a busy and often congested road lined with hotels, fast-food restaurants, and strip malls. The best way to experience the laid-back, summer-vacation atmosphere of Petoskey is to park the car and take a walk through the downtown district to Waterfront Park.

For a glimpse at how the other half lives, stop by the development at Bay Harbor, just west of Petoskey on U.S. 31. Bay Harbor occupies a 5-mile stretch of Little Traverse Bay that once contained an abandoned cement plant; mounds of brick, asbestos, and coal waste; and 2.5 million cubic yards of kiln dust. The transformation of this industrial wasteland into a luxury resort community is truly remarkable. Bay Harbor now contains a deepwater harbor and marina, an equestrian club, the twenty-seven-hole Bay Harbor Golf Club, a massive luxury hotel, and the Village at Bay Harbor, an upscale shopping and dining mall. Scattered within the development and alongside the marina are multimillion-dollar homes, cottages, and condominiums.

Northeast of Petoskey along U.S. 31 lies the National Historic Landmark community of the Bay View Association. What began as a tent community organized by the Methodist Church in 1876 soon evolved into a collection of cottages, a hotel, and a chapel, erected to house participants for a summer program of religious talks and sermons. Today the Victorian-style cottages, the lecture and recital halls, and the chapel still serve the educational needs of the greater community through summer-residency programs in subjects ranging from music and voice training to needlepoint and bridge classes. The parklike atmosphere and the college-campus ambiance of Bay View, together with the town's well-maintained Victorian architecture, make the town a great place to unwind from the touristy bustle of nearby Petoskey.

Along the northern shore of Little Traverse Bay you'll find the community of Harbor Springs. The strip malls and chain restaurants that plague other resort towns are absent here. Instead, the five or six blocks that make up the village's downtown are filled with trendy restaurants and upscale clothing and curio shops, all set against a picturesque harbor and marina. Tucked into the hillside that gently rises from the waterfront are beautifully maintained and unique homes, many of which are bed-and-breakfast establishments.

The Ephraim Shay House, designed and built in 1888 by the inventor of the Shay Locomotive, is one of the more unusual homes in Harbor Springs.

What Is a Petoskey Stone?

In the Devonian period, about 350 million years ago, Michigan was a very different place. Instead of the cold, deep lakes and glacially sculpted landscape we know today, Michigan was covered by a shallow, warm sea filled with the ancestors of modern plants and animals. In this primordial sea lived a species of coral called *Hexagonaria percarinata*.

As the forces of nature raised the seabed up, the colonies of *Hexagonaria* died off and were buried in deep layers of sand and earth. Over time, the sand and earth became rock, and the skeletons of the coral became fossilized, leaving their intricate design embedded in the newly formed stone. When the glaciers passed over Michigan, the fossilized rock was broken apart and scattered over the northwest portion of the Lower Peninsula. Today, the fragments of rock containing *Hexagonaria* are called Petoskey stones—the state stone of Michigan. Searching for Petoskey stones among the pebbles and rocks on upper Lake Michigan's shore is a favorite pastime.

An unpolished Petoskey stone hidden among the stones of a pebble beach may be hard to spot at first, but that is half the fun. With a little practice, picking out a Petoskey becomes much easier. If you're still not having any luck, stop in at one of the area's gift shops and sort through their polished stones for one to your liking. The Little Traverse Historical Museum in Petoskey has an amazing 300-pound Petoskey stone on display.

The house was built in the shape of a hexagon, and it has six wings opening out from a central core that is topped with a tower. The walls of the house, both inside and outside, are composed of stamped steel. An ingenious man with eccentric tastes, Ephraim Shay built and operated the town's waterworks, and he built a 40-foot-long all-steel boat named the *Aha*.

North of Harbor Springs, State Highway M119 twists and turns past homes and cottages until the trees begin to crowd the road, and it slowly becomes enclosed under a forest's canopy. This route is the famous Tunnel of Trees, one of Michigan's premier scenic drives. The two-lane blacktop road passes through the twilight of the beech-maple forest for nearly 20 miles until it breaks out at Cross Village onto a high bluff overlooking Lake Michigan. Spring and autumn are the best times to experience this scenic drive; mid-October usually offers peak fall color.

Cross Village is located at the site of an Ottawa encampment that predates European settlement. The big draw to Cross Village today is Legs Inn, a restaurant specializing in Polish food. The inn's dining area is decorated with unique woodcarvings and polished driftwood, and the top of the building's exterior walls are lined with the iron legs from wood-burning stoves. Along with the inn and a few houses, Cross Village is home to an antique store and gas station. An alternate return route to Harbor Springs is County Road 77, which passes through open farm country and a portion of the Hardwood State Forest.

Downtown Suttons Bay's nineteenth-century buildings have been converted into shops, art galleries, and restaurants.

FACING PAGE, CLOCKWISE FROM THE TOP:
Step back into the world of a nineteenth-century fishing village at Fishtown, a collection of period buildings along a wooden dock in the town of Leland.

The Grand Traverse Lighthouse Museum in Leelanau State Park features tours of a fog-signal building and the Grand Traverse Lighthouse in a nicely landscaped setting at the tip of the Leelanau Peninsula.

Artifacts of Lake Michigan's fisheries decorate Fishtown in Leland, where you can purchase freshly caught fish or charter a fishing trip.

THE LEELANAU PENINSULA

ROUTE 15

From State Highway M72 west of Traverse City, follow State Highway M22 west toward Suttons Bay and Northport. At Northport, follow County Road 201 to County Road 629, then take County 629 north to Leelanau State Park. Backtrack to Highway M22 West and follow it to Leland.

The Leelanau Peninsula extends into Lake Michigan like a protective arm, holding back the tempestuous swells of this Great Lake and calming the waters of Grand Traverse Bay. Our tour of the Leelanau begins at Traverse City, the bustling town at the bottom of Grand Traverse Bay. From State Highway M72, follow State Highway M22 up the eastern edge of the peninsula toward the town of Suttons Bay. The tempo of life slows perceptively as you follow Highway M22 along the sparkling waters of Grand Traverse Bay. This is serious vacation country, so set your pace to the sailboats gliding over the water and relax. It seems the thing to do.

The Leelanau Peninsula is a beautiful slice of land. Named by the native Chippewa, Leelanau means "land of delight," and with its sandy beaches, rolling hills, contoured dunes, clear lakes, and friendly people, the name seems proper and fitting. Many artists call the peninsula home, as do farmers, innkeepers, fishermen, vintners, and retirees.

The Grand Traverse area is premier farm country, renowned for its cherry crop. Both sweet and tart varieties of cherries thrive here. Orchards shimmer with white cherry blossoms in the spring, and roadside stands overflow with bushels and baskets of ripe fruit at harvest time. Michigan produces 70 to 75 percent of the nation's tart cherries, and half of the crop comes from the Grand Traverse area. Another agricultural product of Leelanau that is gaining international acclaim is wine. The sandy, well-drained soil; the moderate climate stemming from the nearness of Lake Michigan; and the peninsula's latitude, 45° north (the same latitude as the Bordeaux region of France and the wine country of Oregon)—all work together to produce a robust crop of grapes. The Leelanau Peninsula Vintners Association represents eleven wineries clustered on the peninsula. Each winery has a tasting room where you can sample the fruits of its labor while enjoying a view of its hillside vineyards.

The village of Suttons Bay has seen tremendous changes since the 1880 census counted 250 inhabitants, but population growth has not been one of them. With only 589 residents counted in the 2000 census, Suttons Bay remains a true small town. The village was founded in 1854 by Harry Sutton, a shoe repairman who would later become the village's first schoolmaster, first postmaster, and village doctor. Over the years, Suttons Bay has seen lumber mills, a fruit processing plant, and plans for a national university come and go. Today, Suttons Bay is a thriving artist and tourist community with a strong sense of its colorful history.

St. Joseph's Avenue, the town's main thoroughfare, is home to an array of art studios, restaurants, gift shops, and specialty shops, many of which are housed in nicely restored nineteenth- and early-twentieth-century buildings. The Citizens Telephone Company Building from the early 1900s is now home to the Michigan Artists Gallery, which features the work of some of Michigan's best-known artisans. Pick up the "Walking History Tour of the

Village of Suttons Bay" brochure at the chamber of commerce for a guided walk past many of the village's historical sites. Summer brings the Suttons Bay community to life with a classic boat show in June, Jazzfest in July, and the Suttons Bay Art Festival in August.

Near the tip of the "little finger" of Michigan's mitten is the village of Northport, built around the natural harbor created by the Northport Point Peninsula. The village was established as an Indian mission in 1849 and originally known as Waukazooville, named after Chief Peter Waukazoo of the Ottawa nation. Things changed quickly as white settlers arrived, and in 1854 the town was renamed Northport.

Northport's harbor offered protection from Lake Michigan's storms, and the surrounding countryside supplied cordwood for ships' steam engines. As timber was depleted, agricultural products—particularly potatoes—replaced lumber as Northport's main commodity. Fruit crops such as cherries, peaches, strawberries, apples, and grapes have since replaced potatoes as the area's main export. The harbor remains a popular stopover for Great Lakes vessels, although most are now pleasure craft drawn to the port by the recreational opportunities of the northern Leelanau Peninsula.

Northport is a quiet village of tree-lined streets, a small downtown, and a waterfront park built around a large municipal marina. Many professional artists live and work here, and their galleries and workshops can be found in homes and storefronts throughout the town. Friday evenings in June, July, and August, the town and its guests turn out for "Music in the Park" at Haserot Park on the waterfront.

After spending only a short time on the Leelanau Peninsula, you wonder what would bring someone to want to leave. For Clinton Woolsey, the desire to serve his country in World War I and the chance to pilot an aircraft led him to far-off places and into the company of many of America's early aviation heroes. Woolsey grew up on a dairy farm outside Northport and left town to become a pilot for the U.S. Army during World War I. His aviation skills led him to remain in the army after the war, and he eventually joined a team of pilots who toured the world promoting American aviation. Woolsey was killed in a midair collision in Buenos Aires in 1927, during a goodwill tour of South America. In memory of his son, Woolsey's father donated the family dairy farm to the township to be used as an airport.

With a 3,600-foot sod runway and a fieldstone terminal (originally the Woolsey dairy barn), Woolsey Memorial Airport still functions as a working airfield. Each year in August the Northport Pilots Association hosts a fly-in/drive-in breakfast at the airfield to raise money for maintenance and repairs. The airfield is located on County Road 629, a few miles north of Northport.

North of Woolsey Memorial Airport, County Road 629 leads to Leelanau State Park and the Grand Traverse Lighthouse at the tip of the peninsula. The 1,300-acre state park is split into two portions: the upper portion at the tip of the peninsula and the larger southern portion along the Lake Michigan

Many galleries and fine-art studios can be found along U.S. Highway 31 between Traverse City and Charlevoix.

Wood anemone thrives in the moist woods at the Torch Bay Nature Reserve in Torch Bay Township.

Clinch Park on the Traverse City waterfront is a great place to fly a stunt kite.

shore. The southern portion is largely undeveloped and features 1.5 miles of sandy Lake Michigan shoreline. Six miles of hiking trails lead through the park's dunes and forests. The upper portion of the park contains a rustic campground adjacent to the Grand Traverse Lighthouse and Museum. The rocky beach near the lighthouse is a great place to hunt for Michigan's official state stone, the Petoskey stone.

Did you ever want to be a lighthouse keeper? The Grand Traverse Lighthouse and Museum offers a program in which interested patrons can live and work at the lighthouse for a week or two. A synopsis of the program and an application are available at the lighthouse. For those interested only in a short visit, the lighthouse and museum are set on a nicely manicured plot of land at the very tip of the Leelanau Peninsula. A nicely restored fog-signal building houses nautical exhibits and a restored foghorn.

Our final stop on the tour of the Leelanau Peninsula lies between Lake Michigan and Lake Leelanau on the sunset coast of the peninsula. Backtrack down County Road 629 to Highway M22 and head west toward the village of Leland. Once a large village of the Ottawa people, Leland was known to the Ottawa as *Mishi-me-go-bing*, which roughly translates as "the place where canoes run up into the river to land, because they have no harbor." Today, arriving boats have the convenience of a breakwater and the municipal harbor to safely dock at Leland. Like so many of the villages on the peninsula, Leland caters to tourists and has fine restaurants, galleries, and gift shops. But it is historic Fishtown on Leland's waterfront that sets this village apart from the others.

Built along the mouth of the Carp River, which connects Lake Michigan and Lake Leelanau, Fishtown is a rustic wooden pier with a collection of buildings, housing fisheries, charter services, and shops. Well-weathered tugs are moored next to modern vessels at a dock where fishing nets dry on wooden spools. If the breeze from Lake Michigan carried the tang of saltwater, you would be convinced that you were visiting a New England fishing village. From the dock at Fishtown, you can purchase fresh or smoked fish, or catch a boat ride to North or South Manitou islands with families who have sailed the waters of Lake Michigan for many generations.

EASTERN GRAND TRAVERSE BAY: TRAVERSE CITY TO CHARLEVOIX

ROUTE 16

Follow State Highway M72 east along the shore of Grand Traverse Bay through Traverse City. At U.S. Highway 31, head north toward Charlevoix.

Reverend Peter Dougherty came to Grand Traverse in 1839 as a Presbyterian missionary to the Chippewa, but it was his cherry trees that forever changed the Traverse Bay region. In 1852, against the advice of many in the farming community, Dougherty planted an orchard of cherry trees on Mission Peninsula. To everyone's surprise, the trees flourished, and forty years later the first commercial cherry orchard was planted nearby. The cherry capital of the world had been born.

Traverse City celebrates the fruits of Dougherty's labors each year at the National Cherry Festival. The festival sprang from the "Blessing of the Blossoms" ceremony, first celebrated in spring 1925. In 1938, the ceremony was renamed the National Cherry Festival and moved from springtime to the month of July. Since then, the popularity of the festival has grown tremendously; it now draws visitors from around the country to an eight-day celebration of everything cherry.

Another man with a mission, who had a profound influence on Traverse City's development as a tourist destination, was Conrad Foster. As parks commissioner in the 1930s, "Con" Foster envisioned a park along the waterfront at the southern tip of West Grand Traverse Bay. The area had been the home of the Hannah Mill, and under Foster's direction, volunteers cleaned up the mess the abandoned mill had left behind.

Foster's volunteers also helped build a small zoo, a beach house, and a museum along the newly restored waterfront. Meanwhile, Foster traveled throughout the Midwest collecting artifacts for the museum, and he soon had a collection of over ten thousand Native American and pioneer-era relics. In 1998, the contents of the museum were relocated to the Carnegie Library Building on Sixth Street, where they became part of the Grand Traverse Heritage Center collection. A zoo, a marina, and a public park with a picnic area and sandy beach still draw locals and tourists to Foster's waterfront.

U.S. Highway 31 from Traverse City to Charlevoix follows the eastern shore of Grand Traverse Bay past orchards, nurseries, and fruit markets of every size and description. The Grand Traverse arts community has a strong presence here; sculptors, painters, potters, and other artisans have shops and galleries tucked away behind homes and along the roadside all along this route. Small towns such as Elk Rapids offer a chance for a walk along a picturesque waterfront, a meal at a family-owned restaurant, or a visit to a shop or gallery, all against the backdrop of manicured lawns, spotless streets, and the sky blue water of Grand Traverse Bay.

If a more natural setting is to your liking, visit the small (40-acre) Torch Bay Nature Preserve in Torch Lake Township. Watch for the sign on the west side of U.S. 31 at Traverse Bay Road. This diminutive reserve offers much to explore, including a stretch of undeveloped Lake Michigan shoreline; hiking trails through wetlands and forests of cedar, balsam fir, and hemlock; and a dune hardwood community of beech, maple, ash, and oak trees. Wildflowers, including trillium, dwarf lake iris, and swamp rose mallow, are also abundant here, especially along Traverse Bay Road.

The town of Charlevoix is a pleasing mix of upscale resorts, well-kept homes, and a Great Lakes port town—all with an undeniable fancy for the unusual. Modern condominiums surround the town's marina on Lake Charlevoix, and the business district bustles with trendy shops and restaurants. The town's neighborhoods, especially those in the older areas between Lake Michigan and Lake Charlevoix, are filled with Victorian-era homes and

The fanciful stone cottages and homes built by Earl Young lend a sense of whimsy to Charlevoix's neighborhoods.

The drawbridge at U.S. Highway 31 in Charlevoix allows tall ships passage between Lakes Charlevoix and Michigan.

The Charlevoix Lighthouse guides sailors, fishermen, and boaters to safe harbor.

charming churches sporting steeples and stained-glass windows. Interspersed among the wood-frame and fieldstone homes are wonderfully unique cottages and homes designed by Earl Young. A real-estate trader by profession, Young had a fancy for stone and a flair for whimsical design. The walls of his creations are made of stones of every size—from massive boulders to fist-sized beach stones—and the roofs are cedar-shake "mushroom caps." Tucked away amongst the neighboring Victorian homes, Young's stone and cedar houses have a decidedly "Middle Earth" air about them. Look for examples of Young's work on Grant Street between Park and Clinton streets, west of downtown Charlevoix.

One of the more peculiar chapters in Michigan history occurred in Charlevoix County in the mid-nineteenth century. When Joseph Smith, the founder of the Mormon Church, was murdered in an Illinois jail, a power struggle for leadership of the Mormons developed between Brigham Young and another elder named James Jesse Strang. Young eventually claimed the title of leader of the church and excommunicated Strang. Young then led the Mormons to Utah, while Strang and his followers settled on Beaver Island, off the coast of Charlevoix. Trouble began when Strang proclaimed himself "King of the Kingdom of God on Earth" and began holding the non-Mormon residents of Beaver Island to strict religious laws. In a short time, Strang succeeded in driving all dissenters to his regime off of the island.

Strang was an influential leader with a large number of followers, and through political means he was soon able to legally enforce his agenda on the larger population of Charlevoix County. He vigorously opposed the liquor trade, even though many fishermen and traders in the area supplemented their meager incomes selling spirits. One group of Irish fishermen who had been forced off Beaver Island by Strang and his followers thumbed their noses at Strang's liquor laws and vowed to shoot anyone who tried to enforce them. When Strang sent the sheriff to arrest the dissenters, the fishermen opened fire, wounding six members of the posse and sending the lawmen scurrying to their boats in full retreat. Not satisfied to drive them off, the fishermen pursued the lawmen out into Lake Michigan, firing at them as they tried to escape.

Strang made many enemies during his often tyrannical governance as "King of Beaver Island," and his reign did not last long. In 1856, a group of men ambushed and shot Strang as he walked along the wharf at St. James Harbor. He died of his wounds several days later, but not before a mob descended on Beaver Island, burning the settlement and deporting his devotees. Without its charismatic leader, and with its adherents scattered, the Mormon sect led by Strang eventually disappeared.

SLEEPING BEAR DUNES NATIONAL LAKESHORE

A Chippewa legend says that long ago, in the land that today is called Wisconsin, a mother bear and her two cubs were driven into Lake Michigan by a raging forest fire. The cubs swam strongly, but the distance was too great and they slipped beneath the waves just before reaching the safety of the opposite shore. When mother bear reached shore, she climbed to the top of a bluff and looked back over the lake, waiting for her cubs. The Great Spirit took pity on her and raised two islands to mark the place her cubs vanished, and then it laid a peaceful slumber on mother bear. The "Sleeping Bear" is a solitary dune overlooking Lake Michigan, and North Manitou and South Manitou islands mark the spots where the cubs perished.

Many years ago, when the great ice glaciers melted back into what is now called Canada, they left behind huge piles of rock and sand and great pools of water. Many years passed, and the level of the waters rose and fell. The currents of the water swept great amounts of sand onto the eastern shore of the lake we now call Michigan, and the prevailing winds piled the sand into low bluffs. The people who later lived on that shore would call these low, sandy hills "beach dunes." The great piles of sand that were left high above the shore when the glaciers melted would be known as "perched dunes." Sleeping Bear is a perched dune.

However you believe the Sleeping Bear Dunes were created, there is no doubt that they are worthy of their national lakeshore status. Stretching for 35 miles along the shore of Lake Michigan, the park encompasses over 71,000 acres of land, including North Manitou and South Manitou islands. Within the park's boundaries you'll find a diverse and spectacular landscape of rolling dunes, towering sand bluffs, crystal-clear lakes and streams, and hardwood forests. All points of interest in the park can be reached via one of two main routes: State Highway M22 or State Highway M109.

From the town of Frankfort on the shores of Betsie Lake, follow Highway M22 north around the western shore of Crystal Lake. North of the small town of Crystallia, just past the yacht club, watch for Point Betsie Road, and turn left toward Lake Michigan. At the end of the road you will find the Point Betsie Lighthouse. The light's classic look and scenic location make it a popular tourist stop and one of the most photographed lighthouses in the United States. Point Betsie also offers a popular beach for windsurfing and for watching the sun set over Lake Michigan.

Beyond Point Betsie, Highway M22 follows Crystal Lake for a few more miles, then turns away from the lake and enters Sleeping Bear Dunes National Lakeshore. This portion of Highway M22 winds through deep forests

ROUTE 17

From State Highway M115 in Frankfort, follow State Highway M22 north toward Crystallia. To visit the Point Betsie Lighthouse, turn west on Point Betsie Road just north of Crystallia. Continue north on Highway M22 to Sleeping Bear Dunes National Lakeshore. At the town of Empire, turn east on State Highway M72 to reach the Philip A. Hart Visitor Center and the park headquarters. To continue through the park, follow Highway M22 north to State Highway M109. At this point, Highway M109 leads to the Pierce Stocking Scenic Drive, the dune climb, Sleeping Bear Point, and the town of Glen Haven. Highway M22 leads north across the causeway on Glen Lake to the town of Glen Arbor. At Glen Arbor, Highway M22 continues north through the remainder of the park.

FACING PAGE:
A wooden walkway leads visitors to the overlook at Empire Bluffs in Sleeping Bear Dunes National Lakeshore.

LEFT:
A group of tubers enjoy their ride down the Platte River in Sleeping Bear National Lakeshore.

BELOW:
Thunderstorms form over Glen Lake in this view from the Cottonwood Hiking Trail near the Pierce Stocking Scenic Drive.

of birch, maple, and oak, occasionally interrupted by grassy meadowlands. Where Highway M22 crosses the Platte River, you'll find a U.S. Forest Service campground, a well-maintained picnic area, and a private outfitter that rents canoes and kayaks for leisurely paddles down the Platte River to Lake Michigan. For those who would rather drive, Lake Michigan Road leads down to the mouth of the river at Platte River Point.

The park headquarters and the Philip A. Hart Visitor Center can be found a few miles north of the Platte River in the town of Empire. Hart was a U.S. senator who represented Michigan in Congress from 1959 until 1976. In the early 1960s, when the unemployment and poverty level of the Upper Great Lakes region rivaled that of Appalachia, Hart proposed a bill that would create a national park at Sleeping Bear. Despite the cheery promises from federal officials that the park would bring tourists with much-needed money into the region, the bill immediately faced fierce opposition from citizens and area business groups. Images of crowded highways and touristy strips like those found in Gatlinburg at the entrance to the Smokey Mountains National Park haunted locals.

The threat of private-property seizure to create the park and the loss of local control of the land to the National Park Service fed a frenzy of resistance. Most local people wanted to preserve the dunes from development, but the attempt by the federal government to do so by creating a national park was seen as a political "land-grab." After a number of attempts and many compromises, the bill creating Sleeping Bear Dunes National Lakeshore became law in 1970.

From Empire, continue north on Highway M22 to where it intersects with Highway M109. Turn left onto Highway M109 and follow it north to Pierce Stocking Scenic Drive. Pick up an informational brochure at the entrance to this scenic drive and make sure to have a camera handy, because this 7.4-mile drive is packed with spectacular overlooks and scenery that rivals anything found in Michigan.

Pierce Stocking was a lumberman from Cadillac, Michigan. Beginning in the 1940s, he purchased land parcels in the Sleeping Bear Dunes area and on South Manitou Island. Many residents feared Stocking would log or develop his holdings on the dunes, but the beauty of Sleeping Bear worked its magic on him. He instead built a house on the dunes overlooking Lake Michigan. In 1967, he finished a scenic road through his extensive property, allowing the public to visit some of the grand vistas and to enjoy the scenery he had come to love. Stocking operated the road until his death in 1976, and a year after he passed away, the scenic drive became part of the national lakeshore.

The road named for Stocking begins with a drive past long rows of tall "plantation pines." Plantations of white and red pines are common in Michigan, especially in areas affected by erosion after logging operations stripped the land of its tree cover during the nineteenth-century timber boom. Beyond the grove of plantation pines, the road passes through a great example of a native-Michigan beech-maple forest. Unlike the dense pines, this forest supports a large number of animals and birds. As you are traveling this route, watch for white-tailed deer, black squirrel, porcupine, ruffed grouse, wild turkey, and even black bear. This area also supports cougars, although they are very rare and seldom seen. Still, it pays to read and heed the warning signs, posted throughout the park, that describe how to react if confronted by one of these big cats.

As Pierce Stocking Scenic Drive winds uphill, out of the forest, and along the edge of the sand dunes, several spectacular vistas open up. Well-maintained overlook platforms offer views of Glen Lake, the Sleeping Bear, the D. H. Day Farm and its spire-topped white barn, Lake Michigan, and Bar Lake. For a close-up look at the dunes, take a walk on the 1.5-mile-long Cottonwood Trail. The trailhead is a short drive past the Dune Overlook pull-off. While the trail is strenuous at times, it is well marked and leads past many unique features and interesting plants.

Walking off-trail and climbing the dunes in Sleeping Bear are discouraged for a number of reasons. The dune ecosystem is a tenuous one of shifting sand and extremes in wind and temperature. The grasses and other plants that stabilize the dunes often fight a losing battle against the elements. Foot traffic complicates the problem by dislodging mounds of sand, causing erosion. Several large "sandslides" have occurred in recent years, sending tons of sand crashing into Lake Michigan.

Climbing dunes is hard work; one step forward is often followed by two sliding steps backward. If you must climb a dune, head north on Highway M109 a short distance from Pierce Stocking Scenic Drive, to the dune-climb area. There you can park your car in the lot facing a one-hundred-foot-tall dune and have at it. Remember to be aware of your physical limitations, wear shoes, and, if you do make it to the top, don't try to run full-speed back downhill. The top of the sandy slope offers a good view of Glen Lake to the east. To the west, the plateau of sand extends for about 4 miles to a 400-foot bluff overlooking Lake Michigan.

After you've emptied your shoes of sand and you've caught your breath, continue north on Highway M109 toward Glen Haven. The town of Glen Haven consists of a collection of buildings owned by the park service. If you're visiting during the summer, stop by the 1920s-era Glen Haven General Store for a look at what tourists were buying during the Roaring Twenties. The town also features a working blacksmith shop and the Cannery Boathouse, an old cannery filled with historic boats and other nautical artifacts. The shortest Michigan highway, half-mile-long State Highway M209, leads from Glen Haven to the Sleeping Bear Point Coast Guard Station/Maritime Museum. At the museum, you can witness reenactments of U.S. Life-Saving Service rescue techniques, review the history of Great Lakes shipping, and experience the firing of a Lyle gun.

One of two campgrounds found at Sleeping Bear, the D. H. Day Campground is located just outside Glen Haven. With limited comfort facilities, D. H. Day caters to those seeking a rustic camping experience. The drive-in

The lighthouse at Point Betsie is loved by photographers and sight-seers for its classic design and beautiful setting.

The spire-topped barns of the D. H. Day Farm are visible from the overlook at Pierce Stocking Drive, from the top of the Dune Climb, or from State Highway M109.

The bright red building that once housed the Glen Haven Canning Company is now a museum dedicated to the vessels that sailed the waters of the Great Lakes.

A wind surfer catches the breeze at Point Betsie.

campground is heavily wooded, creating an atmosphere of privacy and seclusion. Easy access to a Lake Michigan beach, along with the beautiful setting, make the lack of amenities at the campground seem inconsequential.

Just east of the D. H. Day Campground, Highway M109 ends at Highway M22 in the town of Glen Arbor. A thriving tourist town, Glen Arbor sports a collection of upscale galleries and shops, restaurants, bed-and-breakfast inns, cottages, and resort hotels in a picturesque setting between Glen Lake and Sleeping Bear Bay on Lake Michigan. A short drive to the south on Highway M22 takes you to the bridge across the narrows between Big Glen and Little Glen lakes. To the north, Highway M22 passes through a remote section of the park on its way toward Leland. Access roads along the way lead to several interesting hiking trails, including the Bay View Trail, Pyramid Point Trail, and a trail along Good Harbor Bay. If you wish to visit North Manitou or South Manitou islands, a ferry service is available in Leland.

DUNES, BEACHES, AND ART: SAUGATUCK/DOUGLAS TO SOUTH HAVEN

ROUTE 18

From exit 41 on Interstate 196/U.S. Highway 31, take the Blue Star Memorial Highway (also called A2) south toward Saugatuck/Douglas. To visit Saugatuck State Park, turn north on Sixty-fourth Street and then west on 138th Avenue; otherwise, follow the Blue Star Memorial Highway into Saugatuck. From downtown Saugatuck, follow Washington Road along Kalamazoo Lake back to the Blue Star Memorial Highway and turn right (south). Follow the Blue Star Memorial Highway across the Kalamazoo River to Douglas, or follow it all the way to South Haven.

Time blends fact and fiction into legend, and even if the legends are only half true, they often become a part of a town's life story as they are passed from generation to generation. The fact is, America's most notorious gangster, Al Capone, may never have visited Saugatuck, preceded by an advance guard of machine-gun-toting thugs riding shotgun on the car's running board. And the bullet holes in the walls and ceiling of Saugatuck's Twin Gables Hotel may have a less sinister source than drunken, bored gangsters trying to hammer in a protruding nail with hot lead. Legend has it that the stories are true, but only the tin panels of the hotel's walls know the truth, and they aren't talking.

Despite the fondness that Prohibition-era mobsters allegedly held for the town, Saugatuck is a city that has grown up right. Modern-day Saugatuck is alive with art, culture, and style. The trendy studios and shops of downtown, the internationally acclaimed Ox-Bow summer school of art, and the great natural beauty surrounding the city draw visitors from around the world. Saugatuck and its neighbor across the Kalamazoo River, Douglas, form the heart of the "Art Coast of Michigan."

The towns of Saugatuck and Douglas once had a neighbor—the mill town of Singapore. Built on the sand dunes of Lake Michigan at the mouth of the Kalamazoo River, Singapore experienced a brief spike in growth after the great Michigan and Chicago fires of 1871 created an immediate need for lumber. The demand for rebuilding material soon outstripped supply, and by 1875 many of Singapore's buildings were being torn down and moved. The shifting dunes of Lake Michigan smothered the remains of the town, including its cemetery, leaving only an occasional rooftop protruding from the sand.

This old Town of Singapoor has been completely covered with sand 15 to 30 ft. deep, Saugatuck, Mich.

The once thriving mill town of Singapore at the mouth of the Kalamazoo River was partially torn down and moved when local timber supplies ran out. Anything that was left behind was soon buried beneath the shifting dunes of Lake Michigan. Courtesy of State of Michigan Archives/negative #00199

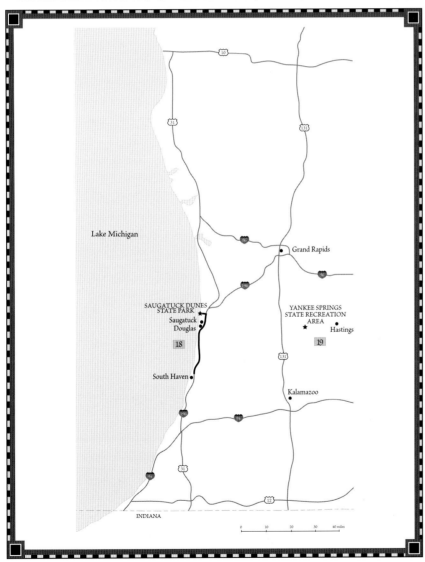

*Every detail has been faithfully repro-
duced on the ship* Friends Good Will.
*The ship is modeled after a British
sloop captured by America's Admiral
Perry in the War of 1812.*

The Friends Good Will, *a replica of
an eighteenth-century sloop, sails into
Lake Michigan from her home port at
the Michigan Maritime Museum in
South Haven.*

ABOVE:
The Keewatin, *a passenger steamship that sailed the Great Lakes from 1907 until 1965, is part of the Keewatin Maritime Museum in Douglas.*

LEFT:
Downtown Saugatuck's streets and alleys are filled with art galleries.

The town of Singapore has not been the only enterprise tested by the sands of Lake Michigan. The USS *Keewatin*, a 1907 coal-fired steamship, spent several months stuck on a sandbar in the Kalamazoo River after a failed attempt to make it up the river to Kalamazoo Lake. The ship was eventually freed and now is safely and permanently moored on the Douglas side of Kalamazoo Lake, just south of the Saugatuck-Douglas Bridge. From Memorial Day to Labor Day, visitors can enjoy a tour of this classic Great Lakes passenger ship.

Just north of Saugatuck is the relatively new and still uncrowded Saugatuck Dunes State Park. The park's only amenities are a small picnic area, a couple of outhouses, and a parking area, but what the 1,100-acre park lacks in services, it more than makes up for in scenic beauty. Several well-maintained walking trails lead through a mature dune forest of maple, American beech, white pine, and red pine. All trails lead to a 2-mile-long stretch of secluded Lake Michigan shoreline. Behind the gold-colored, wave-sculpted sandy beach, the tree-topped Saugatuck dunes rise 150 vertical feet. Often your only beachcombing companions are the soaring gulls and terns that patrol the surf in search of a meal. The spectacular beach and quiet trails at Saugatuck Dunes State Park are a welcome respite from the bustle of nearby Saugatuck and Douglas.

The two-lane Blue Star Memorial Highway (also labeled A2) links Saugatuck/Douglas to South Haven and was once the main north-south thoroughfare between the cities. Nowadays most commercial traffic uses U.S. Highway 196, a modern four-lane highway that shadows the older road. For those interested in a closer look at the local scenery, the Blue Star offers a slower-paced route packed with interesting sights and mom-and-pop businesses. Along the Blue Star are numerous antique dealers, ranging from small, quaint shops to sprawling lawns cluttered with rusting metal curios. Bed-and-breakfast inns (including one for pets), art studios, small restaurants, and plant nurseries are interspersed with fields of highbush blueberry and small farms along the route.

Set between the sandy beach of Lake Michigan and the gently rolling farm country of Southwest Michigan, South Haven sports a population of around six thousand people. Its economy depends largely on a mix of manufacturing, agriculture, and tourism. While downtown South Haven has many businesses geared toward the annual influx of tourists, you can also find stores that sell hardware, clothing, and other everyday amenities. The town's beach is popular with locals and tourists alike, and the South Haven Pierhead Lighthouse, set at the end of a lighted cement jetty, is a favorite subject for photographers, painters, and lighthouse buffs.

For those interested in Great Lakes maritime history, the Michigan Maritime Museum in South Haven has an extensive collection of maritime art, model ships, photographs, historical postcards, maps, and charts. Several restored Coast Guard vessels are also housed at the museum, along with dugout and birchbark canoes, and other artifacts from the early days of travel on the Great Lakes.

The sandy glacial hills of Southwest Michigan are home to a booming wine industry. A visit to a tasting room combined with a stay at a bed-and-breakfast inn, antiquing, gallery hopping, and lounging on the pure sand beaches of southern Lake Michigan is a favorite summer pastime for the urban denizens of nearby Chicago, Grand Rapids, and Detroit. Vintners love the near-perfect growing conditions their grapes enjoy near the shore of Lake Michigan. Cool temperatures in the summer, just the right amount of rainfall, and a moderate winter climate with plenty of snow keep the grape vines happy and the vintners busy. Many of Southwest Michigan's wines enjoy an international popularity that rivals many of the world's more traditional wine-producing areas.

A rescue team works to bring crew members of a grounded freighter safely to shore. Storms and mishaps have caused thousands of shipwrecks on the Great Lakes. Courtesy of State of Michigan Archives

ABOVE:
Fishing is a four-season pastime on the quiet lakes in Yankee Springs Recreation Area.

RIGHT:
A trail leads from a rustic campground to the shore of Deep Lake in Yankee Springs Recreation Area. Facilities at Deep Lake include a boat launch and a fishing pier.

LEFT:
This female northern cardinal is one of many species of songbird that nest in the woodlands of Yankee Springs.

BELOW:
Autumn comes in middle to late October at Yankee Springs. The sugar maple is among the seventy species of tree found in and around Yankee Springs.

ROUTE 19

From U.S. Highway131, take the Bradley exit (129th Avenue/ County Road 430) and head east toward Bradley. West of Bradley, County Road 430 turns south and becomes Gun Lake Road. Follow Gun Lake Road to the Gun Lake campground and day-use area. To reach Hall Lake, continue south on Gun Lake Road. To reach Deep Lake and Turner Lake, continue south to Yankee Springs Road (County Road 611) and turn left. To visit the northern portion of Yankee Springs, follow Yankee Springs Road to Chief Noonday Road (County Road 434) and turn left. Chief Noonday Road will take you back to Gun Lake Road.

Between Kalamazoo and Grand Rapids, where the rolling cornfields give way to forests and clear, quiet lakes, is a place called Yankee Springs State Recreation Area. Steeped in colorful history and awash with natural beauty, Yankee Springs entices visitors with 5,000 acres of public land situated around nine lakes, including a portion of Gun Lake, one of the largest and deepest inland lakes in Michigan. Oak, maple, and hickory trees line the blacktop roads and hang in a green canopy over the narrow sand-and-gravel access roads leading to the park's secluded lakes. Every season offers something new at Yankee Springs.

As it receded ten thousand years ago, the Wisconsin Glacier sculpted the landscape of Yankee Springs. In its wake, the glacier left tall moraines and the many kettle lakes that are found in the park today. Some of the kettle lakes have filled in over the centuries, creating bogs and wetlands that support a variety of interesting plants and animals. One park trail follows the perimeter of the Devil's Soupbowl, a large, deep kettle formation scoured into the ground by a massive chunk of glacial ice.

The modern story of Yankee Springs begins in the early 1800s, as the Napoleonic Wars raged in Europe and the wars' effects rippled through the American frontier. The blockade of Europe, the seizure of American merchant ships by the British navy, and the impressment of American sailors to man British warships eventually boiled over into war between Britain and America, known as the War of 1812. Skirmishes erupted where British-controlled Canada and the American territories of Michigan and Ohio met. Old animosities were rekindled as the native tribes of the region split their alliances between the two warring parties.

Chief Noonday, whose band of Potawatomi lived and hunted in the region around Yankee Springs, chose to fight at the side of the British. Noonday's large physical stature, combined with his influence among the local tribes, made him a great leader. When the famous Pawnee warrior Tecumseh was killed at the Battle of Thames in 1813, it was Noonday who carried his body from the battlefield. Noonday also participated in the British assault on Buffalo, New York, when the city was sacked and burned. After the war, Noonday was instrumental in negotiating the treaties that opened Michigan to settlement. Chief Noonday Lake and an outdoor center in Yankee Springs are named in his honor.

Yankee Springs got its name about twenty years after the War of 1812 ended, when several groups of traveling settlers met by chance at a natural spring. Conversation turned to the adventures they had all faced on the journey to claim land in Michigan. As the conversation progressed, they realized that they were all Yankees from different parts of New England. To commemorate their meeting, a settler named Charles Paul carved the words "Yankee Springs" into an oak tree, and the town was born.

A year after Paul made his mark on the Yankee Springs oak tree, another young man and his family, heading west, decided to end their journey in the area. William Lewis, or Yankee Bill as he would later be called, established a hotel called the Mansion House in Yankee Springs. Situated on the stage route halfway between Grand Rapids and Kalamazoo, the hotel and surrounding settlement soon became the largest town in Barry County.

As the population of settlers expanded, the capacity of the land to support them waned. By the end of the nineteenth century, the forests were largely cut down, the once plentiful wildlife had disappeared, and the poor, sandy soil refused to yield any more crops. By the 1920s, most of the farmers had given up and moved on, and the land lay vacant and eroded. The U.S. Resettlement Administration took control of 4,200 acres in 1934, and soon after, the National Park Service began a land rehabilitation program.

As soon as human pressure was taken off the land, a healing process began. Over 1 million trees were planted, and development began on the hiking trails, beaches, campgrounds, and picnic areas that are found in Yankee Springs today. The State of Michigan took over administration of the park in 1943 and continues to manage things today. As you drive through the rolling forested hills of Yankee Springs, or as you look out over the clear water of its lakes, it's hard to imagine that this was once an ecosystem on the verge of collapse.

One of the most popular destinations in Yankee Springs is the Gun Lake unit, which features a boat launch, picnic area, sand beach, and modern campground. At 2,650 acres, Gun Lake has ample room for all types of watercraft and water sports. It is frequented by fishermen seeking to match wits with bass, panfish, and northern pike. During winter months, ice-fishermen try their luck from inside snug shanties. The modern campground is situated on a nicely wooded site on the lake and includes a bathhouse, RV hookup, and electricity. If a more secluded and rustic camping experience is to your liking, Deep Lake has a large no-frills campground with heavily wooded sites and "primitive accommodations" (outhouses).

For those who would like to stretch their legs or put their stamina to the test, the park offers six hiking trails and 13 miles of the best mountain-bike trails in Southwest Michigan. There are also a horseback camp area and ten miles of riding trails, including a portion of the multistate North Country Trail. During Memorial Day weekend, the Hall Lake Trail is a great spot to view some of the park's plentiful flowering dogwoods in full bloom. You can also take a hike on the Long Lake Trail earlier in the spring for premier wildflower viewing.

If you want to enjoy nature's beauty and ample opportunities for outdoor recreation, then Yankee Springs is a great place to go. The picturesque lakes; the biking, hiking, and horseback-riding trails; the springtime forests decorated with wildflowers and flowering dogwood; and an abundance of wildlife make Yankee Springs a backroad area well worth exploring.

PART IV

UNDER THE THUMB:
SOUTHERN LOWER MICHIGAN

FACING PAGE:
The Huron River flows past a wintry landscape in Hudson Mills Metropark.

ABOVE:
A weathered hickory tree stands along an old fencerow in Waterloo Recreation Area. Large portions of former farmland in Waterloo have been replanted with native grasses and wildflowers.

The people of Michigan love their green spaces, and even though southern Michigan is one of the most urbanized areas in the United States, you can always find a place to hike, swim, fish, or just enjoy the peace of nature nearby. Between southern Michigan's urban centers lies a landscape of rolling farm country dotted with small towns and villages. Within this bucolic landscape are tens of thousands of acres of public recreation area and state and local park land.

Oak-hickory and beech-maple forests dominate southern Michigan. The forested landscape changed dramatically as settlers cleared the land in the late eighteenth century and today, most of southern Michigan's hardwood forests are second growth. The present mixture of farmland and woodlot is excellent habitat for a variety of animals including white-tailed deer, rabbit, wild turkey, and a variety of smaller animals and songbirds.

When European settlers first arrived in southern Michigan to claim farmland, a great many were disappointed by the large areas of marshland and swamp they found. A large portion of southern Michigan's wetlands were eventually drained and turned into farmland, a practice that in many instances caused flooding and other undesirable consequences. Restrictions on development have slowed the loss of wetlands in southern Michigan and the sizeable wetlands that remain still provide a good measure of watershed protection and wildlife habitat.

You are never far from a body of water in southern Michigan; and boating and fishing are favorite summer pastimes. Most lakes in southern Michigan have a public boat launch, even those whose shoreline is lined with private homes and cottages. Public beaches, fishing piers, boat rentals, fishing charters, and bait and tackle shops are plentiful. Fishermen pursue bass, walleye, yellow perch, sunfish, and northern pike in southern Michigan's lakes and rivers, and recreational boaters enjoy touring the regions larger lakes.

OLD US 12: THE IRISH HILLS

ROUTE 20

From the town of Clinton, follow U.S. Highway 12 west toward State Highway M50. Follow Highway M50 east to visit Hidden Lake Gardens, or continue west on U.S. 12 toward U.S Highway 127.

Imagine a place of emerald hills dotted with sky blue lakes. Imagine now that you've left your home in Ireland for the New World and found such a place in the heart of Michigan. Naturally, you would want to call your new home the Irish Hills. In time, people of all backgrounds found that the gentle hills and fifty or so lakes along the Great Sauk Trail were a great place to call home or to escape the pressures of urban life. Today, the Irish Hills are an oasis of vacation homes, tourist attractions, and scenic beauty, just a short drive from most of the large cities in Southeast Michigan.

For as long as there have been people in southern Michigan, they have visited the Irish Hills area. Native Americans traversed a route through the Irish Hills that became known as the Great Sauk Trail. Later, as the populations of Detroit and Chicago grew, the trail became a route for stagecoach and horseback travel between the two cities. The grueling five-day trip by stage was softened for travelers when Sylvester Walker and his wife Lucy erected a three-story brick inn and tavern along the route at Cambridge Junction. The

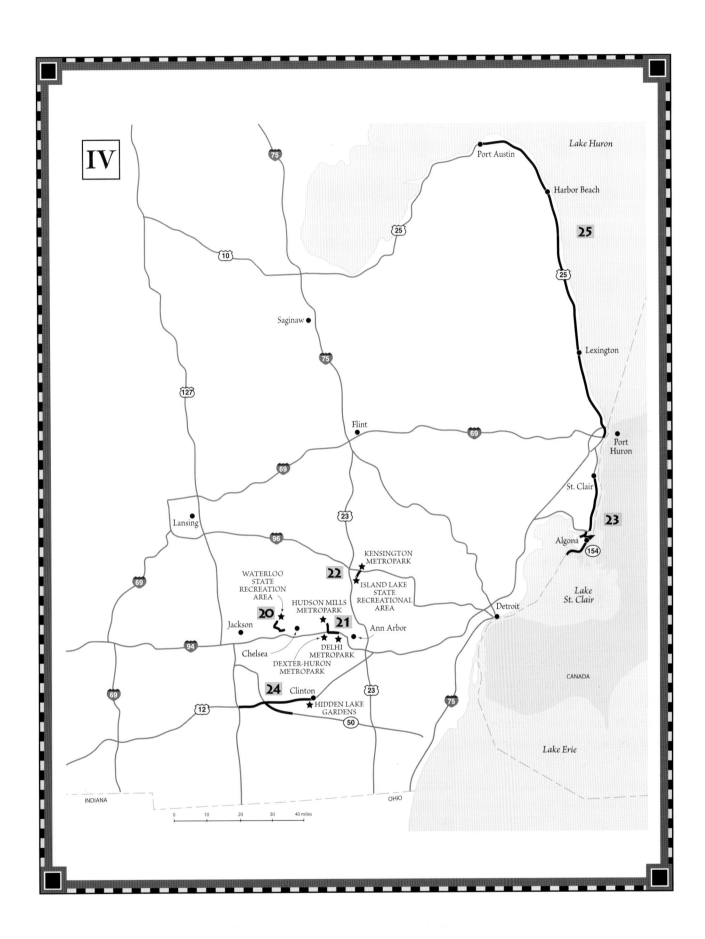

IV

Lake Huron

Port Austin

Harbor Beach

25

25

75

25

10

Saginaw

75

Lexington

127

Flint

69

Port Huron

St. Clair

69

23

69

Lansing

Algona

154

96

Lake St. Clair

KENSINGTON METROPARK

WATERLOO STATE RECREATION AREA

22

ISLAND LAKE STATE RECREATIONAL AREA

HUDSON MILLS METROPARK

20

21

Detroit

Jackson

Ann Arbor

94

Chelsea

DELHI METROPARK

DEXTER-HURON METROPARK

CANADA

69

24

Clinton

HIDDEN LAKE GARDENS

23

12

50

75

Lake Erie

INDIANA

OHIO

0   10   20   30   40 miles

ABOVE:

Beds of annuals surround a small picnic area at Hidden Lake Gardens, a 775-acre botanical garden and arboretum owned by Michigan State University.

RIGHT:

Over 6 miles of paved roadway wind past woodlands, meadows, hosta gardens, and plant collections at Hidden Lake Gardens.

Antique shops along Old U.S.12 in the Irish Hills offer everything from furniture to folk art.

Round Lake in W. J. Hayes State Park beckons to early-rising fishermen hoping to lure a trophy largemouth bass out of its weedy hideout.

Walker Tavern, at the junction of U.S. Highway 12 (the modern name for the Great Sauk Trail) and State Highway M50 in the heart of the Irish Hills, is preserved as part of Cambridge Junction State Historical Park.

The historic tavern and the 80-acre parcel of land surrounding it are the focus of educational exhibits and programs detailing the life and times of Michigan's settlement era. Exhibits at the visitor center tell of the people who have passed through Cambridge Junction over the years. Events such as classic-car shows and a Civil War muster keep things lively at the park during the summer months.

About the same time the tavern was built, the industrious Irish community began construction on a fieldstone church to serve the Irish Hills parish. Built near a historic religious site where Father Gabriel Richard ministered to the local Native Americans, Saint Joseph's Chapel replaced local homes as a place to celebrate mass. A tower and stained-glass windows were added to the church in 1911, and in 1932, work was started on an outdoor garden and walkway depicting the fourteen stations of the cross. Today the church, a small cemetery, and the scenes of the Via Dolorosa still stand overlooking a peaceful lake. On the western end of the church parking lot, you'll find an eloquent monument to the Irish famine.

For a taste of cultivated nature, follow Highway M50 south from Cambridge Junction to the Hidden Lake Gardens in Tipton. A botanical garden operated by Michigan State University, Hidden Lake Gardens is 755 acres of horticultural paradise. Beds of hostas, dwarf and rare conifers, perennials, and annuals surround Hidden Lake, a shallow body of water nestled in the hills like a reflecting pool. A resident family of mute swans adds a final touch of elegance to the pastoral setting.

At Hidden Lake Gardens, 6 miles of one-way blacktop road wind through woodlands and meadows, offering plenty of pull-offs where you can stop and enjoy the garden's many different displays. Five miles of well-maintained hiking trails accommodate those who wish to stretch their legs. The gardens also feature a conservatory with a tropical room (especially nice to visit in the winter), an arid room, and a large collection of orchids and flowering houseplants. A bonsai collection is on display during the summer months, and for a couple days in December, 1,400 hand-lit luminaries are arranged on the grounds in holiday designs.

W. J. Hayes State Park, between Wamplers Lake and Round Lake, is a natural area that caters to the boating, fishing, and beach crowd. One of Michigan's oldest state parks, Hayes was dedicated in 1922 as Cedar Hill State Park. Later, a gift of additional land from the family of state senator Walter Hayes was acknowledged by renaming the park in his honor. A nice beach and a modern campground bring droves of tourists into the park each summer, especially during race weekends at nearby Michigan International Speedway.

At 780 acres, Wamplers Lake is a large body of water perfectly suited to Jet Skis and powerboats. Despite heavy water-sport use, the lake draws plenty of fishermen with the promise of landing largemouth or smallmouth bass, panfish, or northern pike. The smaller, more picturesque Round Lake, near the campground, has a "no-wake" boating policy. With two fishing piers, it is a great spot to cast for bass or panfish without the noise or worry of powerboats.

U.S. 12 has always been a haven for those who enjoy roadside attractions. In 1924, an enterprising businessman built the Irish Hills Observation Tower on the highest parcel of land along the road. The instantly popular tower gave visitors a great scenic view of the lush topography of the Irish Hills. Shortly afterward, a second tower was built by another entrepreneur a few yards from the first tower. The "spite tower," as this second tower became known, sought to siphon off some of the crowds (and profits) from the original tower. Both towers are still standing, but they are in an unfortunate state of disrepair and are therefore temporarily closed to the public. Miniature-golf courses, theme parks, go-cart tracks, and souvenir shops crowd the road in some places, making portions of U.S. 12 feel like a roadside carnival. For the more discriminating traveler or shopper, the area has many quaint and interesting antique, folk-art, and specialty shops to browse during the heat of the day or on a rainy afternoon.

ALONG THE UPPER HURON: HUDSON MILLS, DEXTER-HURON, AND DELHI METROPARKS

Northwest of Ann Arbor, the Huron River runs clean and free through the pastoral farmlands of Southeast Michigan. Along the way, the river's steady current channels through rapids and corridors of forest at Hudson Mills Metropark, murmurs as a gentle riffle at Dexter-Huron Metropark, and jumps over boulder rapids at Delhi Metropark. Accessed from Huron River Drive, the three metroparks were developed at scenic intervals along the Huron River as it meanders from the Pinckney Recreation Area toward the town of Dexter.

Hudson Mills, the largest of the three parks, is located near the intersection of North Territorial Road and Huron River Drive at the site of a former mill. In 1827, Cornelius Osterhout took advantage of the Huron River's steady current and built a sawmill to process the timber that was being cleared by homesteaders. In 1846, a gristmill replaced the sawmill, processing over six thousand barrels of wheat and corn per year from the newly established farms. Later, a cider mill, a pulp mill, and a plaster mill occupied the site, which in time grew to include four homes, a school, a hotel, and a cemetery. Today, all that remains of the mill and the hamlet is the stone wall of the mill, visible on the bank of the river across from the Rapids View Picnic Area.

The Rapids View and River Grove areas in Hudson Mills are two of the nicest places to enjoy a summer picnic in Southeast Michigan. Rapids View Picnic Area is tucked into a small mature wood next to the chattering water of a scenic rapid. A small creek runs through the picnic grounds and empties into the larger flow of the Huron in a swirling whirlpool. In the winter,

ROUTE 21

From the intersection of Dexter-Pinckney Road and North Territorial Road, head east on North Territorial Road 0.5 miles to Hudson Mills Metropark. To reach Dexter-Huron Metropark and Delhi Metropark, follow North Territorial Road east from Hudson Mills Metropark to Huron River Drive and head south.

FACING PAGE, CLOCKWISE FROM THE TOP:
A January hoar frost clings to the trees lining the Huron River. The river's strong current keeps it ice-free during the winter.

A grove of trees in Hudson Mills Metropark glisten in the frosty morning light. The open woods that shade picnickers in the summer provide excellent cross-country skiing in the winter.

Cardinal flowers grow in the muddy floodplain of the Huron River.

LEFT:
The open parkland found in the Upper Huron River metroparks is ideal habitat for the eastern bluebird.

BELOW:
Ground fog glows in the morning light at Hudson Mills Metropark.

the cross-country-ski trail passes through the picnic area and over a small bridge spanning the creek.

River Grove Picnic Area sits in the shade of a mature oak forest along the banks of a pond formed where the Huron's path splits around an island. The pond is a favorite hangout for Canada geese and mallard ducks, and the oak trees host a large number of acrobatic and well-fed squirrels. The park's 3.5-mile-long paved hiking and biking trail passes along the edge of River Grove and over a bridge to the river island. Autumn carpets the ground at River Grove with sweet-smelling fallen oak leaves.

An eighteen-hole, par-71 public golf course occupies most of the park's land on the west side of the Huron River. Access to the course is from Dexter-Pinckney Road, south of North Territorial Road.

From North Territorial Road, head south on Huron River Drive to visit the smaller and more rustic Dexter-Huron Metropark. Along the way, the tree-lined Huron River Drive shadows the river as it winds past well-kept homes and large woodlots. Mid- to late October, when autumn turns the tree canopy gold, is a nice time to enjoy this stretch of road. The route is also popular with bicyclists and joggers, especially on the weekends, so be sure to respectfully share the road.

Dexter-Huron lacks the modern facilities of most of the other metroparks, but what it lacks in convenience, it makes up for in serenity. Against the backdrop of the Huron River's gentle current, visitors can relax on a streamside bench and watch barn swallows and cedar waxwings catch insects over the river. The park's large oak, maple, ash, and sycamore trees harbor an amazing variety of open-woodland birds, including blue jays, orioles, flycatchers, cardinals, nuthatches, woodpeckers, and chickadees. Dexter-Huron's grassy banks are a great place to throw in a fishing line or to launch a canoe for a short downstream run to Delhi.

To reach Delhi by car, continue east on Huron River Drive to East Delhi Road and turn right. A steel-framed wood-plank bridge takes you over the Huron River just below the Delhi Rapids. A quick right turn into a small parking area leads to a canoe rental and a good spot to view the rapids. Turn right on Delhi Court to access the western portion of the park and the canoe take-out. Keep an eye out for bright red cardinal flowers and purple Joe-Pye weed growing alongside the river in late summer. Here, the river begins to pick up speed for its run through a series of boulders and small, rocky islands known as the Delhi Rapids.

Turn left on West Delhi Road to access the park's large, open picnic area and baseball diamonds, or to take a walk along the grassy, willow-lined banks of the river as it bends gently to the south. Follow the river upstream for a great view of the East Delhi Bridge and to watch canoers, kayakers, and tubers run the rapids. The slower currents and shallow water on the downstream side of the rapids attract belted kingfishers and great blue herons, as well as human fishermen, who ply the water for rock bass and sunfish.

An Oasis of Nature:
Kensington Metropark and the
Island Lake Recreation Area

At 4,300 acres, Kensington Metropark near Milford is one of the larger metroparks, and, with over 2 million visitors each year, one of the most popular. Kensington was developed around Kent Lake, in an area that has seen a tremendous boom in both commercial and residential building in the last several decades. The original mission of the metroparks—to provide recreational green space for a burgeoning population—has been realized at Kensington. The all-season park surrounding Kent Lake is an oasis of serenity and outdoor recreation in an increasingly urbanized area of Southeast Michigan.

The main road through the park follows the shoreline of Kent Lake, twisting through oak forests and open meadows and offering several superb panoramas of the island-dotted lake. A very popular, 8-mile-long, 10-foot-wide biking/walking/jogging/inline skating/wheelchair-accessible paved trail roughly parallels the road through the park. The hilly, twisting trail along the lakeshore is well maintained and provides a splendid walk in any season.

A 10-mile-per-hour speed limit for powerboats makes Kent Lake a popular spot for sailboats and other smaller craft. On a weekend afternoon in the summer, it is not unusual to see scores of colorful sailboats tacking over the 1,200-acre lake. Fishermen ply the lake's shallow, weedy bays for bass and northern pike and its deeper waters for crappie and walleye. Ice fishing keeps the action going when the temperatures drop in January and February.

For a nautical tour of the lake, take a ride on the *Island Queen II* excursion boat. The forty-six-passenger boat makes hourly trips each day, leaving from the boat-rental dock. If a more intimate cruise around the lake is to your liking, the park also rents two-person paddleboats. There are several public boat launches for anyone wishing to explore the lake in their own vessel.

Wildwing Lake and the nature-study area in the southeast corner of the park offer incredible wildlife viewing. From the new boardwalk along the eastern shore of the lake, you can observe an active great-blue-heron rookery, an osprey nesting platform, snowy egrets, mute swans, Canada geese, pied-billed grebes, mallard and wood ducks, red-winged blackbirds, sandhill cranes, and many types of raptors and smaller wading birds. Look carefully along the shore for white-tailed deer wading into the water to munch on the succulent vegetation.

North of Wildwing Lake, the Kensington Nature Center is the terminus for several well-maintained hiking trails leading through a variety of habitats. Whichever path you choose, you will be amazed at the variety and number of creatures that you encounter. The white-tailed deer here are numerous and well adapted to the presence of people. As long as they aren't harassed, any

Route 22

From exit 153 on Interstate 96, follow Kent Lake Road north to the toll booth. Follow the road through the park (Park Route 1) to Buno Road and turn west. Buno Road crosses the upper portion of Kent Lake at a bridge and continues west. About 0.75 mile past the bridge, turn south onto Park Route 2 and continue through the park. At the intersection of Park Route 2 and Kensington Road, follow Kensington Road south. The entrance to Island Lake Recreation Area is on the east side of Kensington Road, 0.5 mile south of I-96.

The morning fog envelopes one of Kent Lake's many small islands.

FACING PAGE:
Kent Lake reflects the colors of a summer sunrise. Many joggers, cyclists, and walkers enjoy morning workouts along the paved path that surrounds the lake.

Hot air balloonists launch their gondolas from Island Lake Recreation Area for a ride over the farmland of Southern Michigan.

A white-tailed deer enjoys a meal of succulent water plants in Wildwing Lake. Metroparks such as Kensington provide an excellent habitat for the deer, so much so that overpopulation has become a problem.

deer you encounter will usually continue about their business, completely unconcerned with your presence. Late spring and early summer are good times to search the trails for fawns, and twins are a common occurrence. Encounters with animals, from chipmunks to mink, are common during a quiet walk. Just about every woodland bird found in southern Michigan can be viewed up-close along Kensington's nature trails. Check the nature center building for an up-to-date list of bird sightings.

The natural beauty and abundance of wildlife make the Kensington Nature Center trails favorite spots for photographers. The white-tailed-deer herd of Kensington is probably the most photographed deer herd in Michigan. With the large number of visitors the park receives, a telephoto lens and respect for both the animals and their habitat will help keep nature photography a positive experience for photographers and their subjects.

South of Kensington Metropark you'll find the 4,000-acre Island Lake Recreation Area. A mixture of oak-hickory forest, open brushland, and meadow that surrounds the meandering path of the Huron River, Island Lake Recreation Area caters to all types of outdoor activity. Fishermen will find sunfish and rock bass in the Huron, largemouth and smallmouth bass in the park's lakes, and stocked trout in Spring Mill Pond. Hunting is also popular, and white-tailed deer, cottontail rabbit, goose, and duck are the most popular quarry. When at least 4 inches of snow cover the ground, snowmobilers are welcome to utilize the park's trail system.

During summer and early autumn, hot-air ballooning over the open farm country west of Detroit is a popular pastime. It is not uncommon to see a small fleet of colorful gondolas rising above the trees or hanging over the waters of Kent or Island lakes. The only port from which to launch hot-air balloons within the Michigan park system is located in the Island Lake Recreation Area.

ALONG THE ST. CLAIR RIVER

ROUTE 23

From Interstate 94, follow State Highway M29 toward New Baltimore. Continue to follow Highway M29 along Anchor Bay to Algonac, where it heads north along the St. Clair River toward St. Clair. The ferry to Harsens Island is located off Highway M29 in Algonac.

Despite having more commercial shipping traffic than the Suez and Panama canals combined, and despite being an hour's drive from metropolitan Detroit, the communities along the St. Clair River have maintained the slow-paced, touristy feel of Michigan resort towns. From St. Clair's riverfront park to the Victorian homes of Marine City and to Algonac, the Venice of Michigan, State Highway M29 passes along a water route with a long and colorful history. Early traders and farmers noted that the lakeplain prairie and the oak savannah found along the river were easily converted into farmland.

Even today, the tabletop landscape with rich soil along the river has an easy feel to it. Flat fields of soybean and corn edge up to vast marshlands thick with cattails and canary grass. The banks of the St. Clair are productive for both agriculture and nature. Where the river spills into Lake St. Clair in a fan-shaped delta, the fishery it creates grows trophy walleye, bass, and muskellunge.

A short ferry ride from the town of Algonac takes you to Harsens Island in the heart of the St. Clair River Delta. A large portion of Harsens and neighboring Dickinson Island consists of the St. Clair Flats State Wildlife Area, a huge expanse of marsh and wetlands divided by narrow channels and streams. The delta wetlands are excellent breeding grounds for waterfowl and also support a large population of nongame birds and animals. Three deep channels around Harsens and Dickenson islands keep boat traffic moving between the Upper and Lower Great Lakes.

For freighter watching, it's hard to beat Algonac State Park. The park's modern campground sits along the shoreline of the St. Clair River, separated from the water only by the two blacktop lanes of Highway M29. Park benches along the waterfront provide a front-row seat for the parade of ships passing by on the river. As night falls and campfires are lighted, passing ships take on a larger-than-life character. Green light to bow and red light to stern, their decks outlined in white running lights, the two-story-tall, 200-foot-long ships slip by in the darkness with a deep, diesel-engine hum and a quiet splash from their bow wave.

Algonac State Park also boasts two globally significant and rare ecosystems—a lakeplain prairie and an oak savannah. Of all the nature trails in Michigan's state parks, the Blazing Star Prairie Trail, a rare remnant lakeplain prairie, is one of the shortest (0.5 mile) and easiest to walk, yet in the summer

The Chris-Craft boat company of Algonac was the first manufacturer to mass-produce the runabout, a small mahogany motorboat popular on the Great Lakes. The success of the runabout made Chris-Craft the largest manufacturer of boats in the world. Courtesy of State of Michigan Archives/negative #01198

Wild bergamot and dozens of other native wildflowers flourish at the Blazing Star Prairie Trail in Algonac State Park.

ABOVE:
Over 550 different types of plants have been identified in Algonac State Park, including several species of native thistle.

FACING PAGE, CLOCKWISE FROM THE TOP LEFT:
The canals of Algonac gave rise to the city's nickname, the "Venice of Michigan."

Holy Cross Church in Marine City is built in the classical tradition of the great cathedrals of Europe.

The waterfront in St. Clair along the St. Clair River is a great place to stroll, picnic, or watch Great Lakes freighters pass by.

it is one of the most colorful and lively trails in the state park system. On either side of the mowed-grass path, prairie grasses, some of them reaching 7 or 8 feet in height, intermingle with a colorful riot of wildflowers. Lavender bergamot and blazing star, yellow goldenrod and sunflower, and bright pink milkweed swirl around the deep orange bells of Michigan lily and the tiny blue flowers of blue-eyed grass. Monarch, fritillary, crescent spot, swallowtail, sulpher, and admiral butterflies share the bounty of nectar with bumblebees and exotic-looking hummingbird moths.

Larger than the butterflies and moths, yet just as vibrant, are the birds. Goldfinch and indigo bunting scour the foliage for insects and seeds, while tree swallows snatch meals from the prairie's airspace. Bobolink, with their black-and-white "tuxedo on backwards" markings, nest deep in the grass, guarding their turf with a low-pitched, almost electronic-sounding song.

Equally rare and fascinating is the remnant oak savannah preserved in Algonac State Park. Like the lakeplain prairie, the oak savannah requires periodic burning to remove plants that would eventually change the grasslands to mature forest. In the days before cultivation, lightning fires burned the built-up thatch of the savannahs and prairies and kept the invading forest at bay. Fire-tolerant grasses and oak trees thrived after a fire, while less tolerant species died back. Today, trained members of the Michigan Department of Natural Resources use controlled burns to keep the rare ecosystems intact.

Along St. Clair's Waterfront Park, it's not unusual to see the red and white flags of scuba divers bobbing in the near-shore waters. Beneath the choppy current, the divers pick through the debris of the last one hundred years, searching for small treasures lost, or tossed, in the river. Antique bottles, fishing lures, tools, and other artifacts of the people who live along the St. Clair are sometimes recovered, but the river bottom also holds the remains of Prohibition-era bottled contraband, ditched overboard when the law closed in.

From 1920 until 1933, the St. Clair River was a busy and dangerous place. Prohibition turned sleepy backwater towns along the river into epicenters of liquor smuggling. In the early days of Prohibition, booze-running across the river from Canada into the United States was practiced by anyone with a thirst and a rowboat. But as organized crime and gangs became involved, the situation changed dramatically.

Large-scale smuggling operations, controlled by increasingly ruthless criminals, were set up along the waterway from Port Huron to Detroit. Kidnappings, shootouts, and hijackings became commonplace, often taking place without interference from a police force that was obviously corrupt. The corridor along the St. Clair River, Lake St. Clair, and the Detroit River was so amenable to smuggling that 75 percent of all illegal liquor entering the United States during Prohibition came through this route. With the enactment of the twenty-first amendment repealing Prohibition, the St. Clair River once again became a quiet and safe place, and the search for and retrieval of a bottle of smuggler's whiskey has become merely a prize for sport divers.

WATERLOO RECREATION AREA

The place we now call the Waterloo Recreation Area has, in many ways, come full circle since the land was first converted from wilderness to farmland in the early 1800s. Once a mixture of oak-hickory forest, tamarack and hardwood swamp, bogs, and prairie fens, Waterloo's forests were cleared for farmland or cut for lumber and firewood, and many of its wetlands were drained. Today, the forests have regrown, and much of the former farmland has been replanted with native grasses and wildflowers. Vast wetlands still cover a large portion of Waterloo, helping to support a healthy ecosystem.

Before 1600, the area was frequented by hunting parties of the Potawatomi, Chippewa, Ottawa, and Sauk tribes pursuing elk, black bear, and deer. Settlers first arrived in the 1820s and began cutting forests and draining wetlands to access the rich soil. The rapid deforestation and the diversion of water had the unfortunate side effect of lowering the level of surface water in area lakes by as much as 6 feet.

Homesteading was a risky business, especially in the harsh climate of southern Michigan. The uncertainty of frontier life was driven home hard in the winter of 1834, when particularly cold weather froze both domestic livestock and wild animals alike. The following summer, abnormally dry conditions fostered a plague of grassfires, which threatened the settlers and their homes. The most devastating blow to strike the Waterloo settlers, however, was not wielded by Mother Nature but by the Great Depression of the 1930s. Ironically, the financial tragedy that destroyed the dreams of many local residents also led directly to the formation of the Waterloo Recreation Area.

So many farms were failing due to the hard economic times that in 1934, the U.S. Resettlement Administration began the Waterloo project. The aim was to purchase land that otherwise would be abandoned, and by 1936, twelve thousand acres in the area had been acquired. In 1937, acting in concert with the National Park Service, the Civilian Conservation Corps replanted 1,000 acres of project land with 350,000 trees. The following year—under pressure from locals who were dissatisfied with the way the park service was running things—control of Waterloo was turned over to the State of Michigan.

Modern-day Waterloo is a patchwork of over 20,000 acres of state land interspersed among privately held property and farms. Roads through the recreation area are well maintained year-round, and many are paved, though most that run through the heart of the recreation area are gravel. All public land is clearly posted, as is most private property. Use caution when driving the twisting, turning roads, as Waterloo is a popular destination for walkers, bicyclists, and horseback riders.

Our journey through Waterloo begins in the village of Chelsea, just north of Interstate 94 on State Highway M52. This small but growing community of nineteenth-century homes and newer construction offers many dining, shopping, and antiquing opportunities. The Purple Rose Theatre on

ROUTE 24

From Interstate 94, follow State Highway M52 north to the village of Chelsea. (Highway M52 is called Main Street in Chelsea.) Just north of the railroad tracks in town, turn left onto Sibley Road, then right onto Conway Road, and then left onto Bush Road. When Bush Road crosses Pierce Road, the Waterloo Recreation Area begins. Follow Bush Road to the Gerald Eddy Discovery Center or continue west to McClure Road and turn left. Follow McClure Road to Loveland Road and turn left. At Maute Road, turn right and follow Maute Road to Clear Lake Road. At Clear Lake Road, turn right and drive to Trist Road. Turn left on Trist Road. Trist Road will turn into Seymour Road, which leads to the Big Portage Lake Unit and Campground and the Phyllis Haehnle Memorial Audubon Sanctuary.

Ice breaks up in March on Big Portage Lake in the Waterloo Recreation Area, providing open water for migrating ducks, swans, and geese.

ABOVE:
Trains still run past the Chelsea Depot on their way across Southern Michigan. First constructed in 1880, the depot was restored in the 1980s and now serves as a museum and transportation center for the village of Chelsea.

FACING PAGE:
Coreopsis is one of many wildflowers that flourish in the restored grasslands of Waterloo Recreation Area. Many birds benefit from grasslands, including bobolinks, tree swallows, wild turkeys, and mallard ducks.

Park Street is a great place to see a play featuring some of the finest actors, directors, and playwrights in the Midwest.

On the north end of town, the iconic Chelsea Clock Tower rises over the old Glazier Stove Works Building, which is now home to several businesses, including the Chelsea Teddy Bear Company. You may also wish to tour the nearby Chelsea Milling Company, makers of Jiffy brand muffin mix. Look for the big muffin-mix box west of the clock tower, or just follow your nose.

From Highway M52 north of the clock tower (Highway M52 is called Main Street in town), go west on Sibley Road to Bush Road and turn right (north). Once you cross Pierce Road and the pavement turns to gravel, you have entered the Waterloo Recreation Area. Turn into the Gerald E. Eddy Discovery Center and don your hiking boots for your first taste of Waterloo.

The newly remodeled Discovery Center overlooks Mill Lake to the west. From the viewing deck, two spotting scopes mounted on turrets allow visitors to get a close-up look at Canada geese and a variety of other waterfowl on the lake. The center itself is the hub for information on the Waterloo area, sponsoring a variety of lectures, nature walks, and exhibits throughout the year. Take a few minutes to wander the paved "geology path" behind the center to see specimens of rock from around the state. Five hiking trails start near the center, each passing through a different habitat.

West of the Discovery Center, Bush Road and McClure Road wind past the access sites for Walsh Lake and Mill Lake. Both of these lakes have decent populations of bass and sunfish and are great spots to paddle your canoe or kayak in peaceful surroundings. Mill Lake allows only electric trolling motors, and Walsh Lake is fairly small, so you won't have to contend with Jet Skis or powerboats.

McClure, Maute, and Glenn roads traverse the heart of Waterloo, passing from field to forest, through wetlands and horse pastures, and crossing hiking and horseback-riding trails all along the way. The roadside and surrounding woodlands are resplendent with wildflowers in the spring, including trillium, wild geranium, spring beauty, marsh marigold, and rue anemone. On any warm evening in April or May, park your car near one of the many ponds or wetlands along the road and treat yourself to a chorus of spring peepers, western chorus frogs, gray tree frogs, and wood frogs, as the males sing from the springtime pools. In autumn, sugar maple, red oak, white oak, sassafras, and aspen light up the forest with every shade of red and yellow imaginable.

The Big Portage Lake unit, occupying most of the southern shore of Big Portage Lake, is probably the most visited site in Waterloo. The unit includes a grass and sand beach, a modern campground, a boat launch, a fishing pier, picnic areas, and a seasonal store. Despite its sometimes heavy human use, Big Portage Lake is also visited by large numbers of waterfowl, including buffleheads, scaup, mallards, whistling swans, and Canada geese.

The Waterloo-Pinckney Trail begins adjacent to the boat launch; the trail extends for 22 miles as it winds from Big Portage Lake to Green Lake on the eastern edge of the recreation area.

On the western edge of the Waterloo Recreation Area, about 3 miles west of Portage Lake on Seymour Road, is the 1,000-plus-acre Phyllis Haehnle Memorial Audubon Sanctuary. The original sanctuary land was a gift from Casper Haehnle to the Audubon Society in memory of his daughter Phyllis, and the sanctuary has recently been enlarged with purchases of surrounding properties. The sanctuary is maintained by the Jackson County Audubon Society and not officially part of the recreation area. The Haehnle Sanctuary is well worth the short drive, especially in October and November when hundreds of sandhill cranes congregate each evening in the sanctuary marsh. From a hilltop viewing area, you can watch flocks of the 4-foot-tall cranes fly directly overhead as they head for the sanctuary marsh to roost.

For a glimpse of what life was like in the early to mid-nineteenth century in Waterloo, visit the Waterloo Farm Museum on Waterloo-Munith Road. The site features a fully furnished Victorian farmhouse that was once home to the Realy family, some of the area's earliest settlers. The house is surrounded by many interesting outbuildings, including a blacksmith's workshop, an ice house, a windmill, and a period barn that has been relocated to the site. Tours of the buildings are available for a nominal fee on summer weekends.

THUMBS-UP: PORT HURON TO PORT AUSTIN

The city of Port Huron sits, well weathered and comfortable, at the gateway to the Upper Great Lakes. In the 325 years since the French built Fort St. Joseph at the site of modern-day Port Huron, the city has seen the raw materials and manufactured goods of the Midwest stream past its shore to world markets. Port Huron's sister city, Sarnia, Ontario, lies just across the St. Clair River, linked to Port Huron by the Blue Water Bridge and the world's first submarine rail line, the St. Clair Railroad Tunnel. Lately, Port Huron's importance as a center of cross-border trade with Canada has expanded, as evidenced by the never-ending line of trucks crossing over the Blue Water Bridge.

America's greatest inventor, Thomas Edison, spent his childhood years in Port Huron. Artifacts recovered from Edison's boyhood home (which burned down) can be found at the Port Huron Historical Museum, along with Native American relics and other memorabilia from the city's past. A favorite stop for busloads of schoolchildren visiting the museum is an original log cabin from Port Huron's settlement days. The museum is located near the eclectic mix of vintage and modern buildings of Port Huron's downtown.

Port Huron's nautical heritage is celebrated each year during the last week of July with the kick-off of the Blue Water Festival. The celebration culminates with the launch of the famous Port Huron to Mackinac Island Sailboat Race,

ROUTE 25

From Interstate 94 in Port Huron, follow Highway M25 north toward Lexington. Continue to follow Highway M25 up the coast to Port Austin.

TOP RIGHT:
Built in 1857, Point Aux Barques Lighthouse near Huron City is now a museum featuring photos and artifacts from maritime life on Lake Huron.

BOTTOM RIGHT:
The town of Lexington—a mixture of upscale shops and restaurants, bed-and-breakfast inns, and well-kept homes—is built around a modern marina and park on Lake Huron.

FACING PAGE, TOP:
The Blue Water Bridge connects Port Huron with Sarnia, Ontario. Beneath the bridge, the Thomas Edison Depot Museum is housed inside the historic Fort Gratiot train depot.

FACING PAGE, BOTTOM:
Modern marinas along the shore of Michigan's Thumb provide safe mooring for sailboats, yachts, and fishing boats.

a grueling contest running the length of Lake Huron from Port Huron to Mackinac Island. Lighthouse Park, just north of the Blue Water Bridge, is a great place to watch the contestants leave the safety of the St. Clair River and head north into the waters of Lake Huron.

The Port Huron to Mackinac race consists of two courses: one following the shoreline of Michigan, and the second tracking a longer route around Cove Island in Canada's Georgian Bay. To date, the fastest time for the shoreline course is 25 hours, 47 minutes, and 19 seconds, set in 1950 by the 75-foot-yawl *Escapade*. The *Windquest* holds the Cove Island course record with a blistering time of 26 hours, 41 minutes, and 1 second—an amazing achievement considering the Cove Island course is 55 nautical miles longer than the shoreline course.

North of Port Huron, State Highway M25 passes by several miles of strip malls and fast-food restaurants before the scenery changes to a more rustic setting of lakefronts lined with some amazingly lavish homes and cottages. As the road heads north, the opulent dwellings give way to small resorts and mom-and-pop businesses. At the village of Lakeport, the first of many small towns and villages along Highway M25, you can swim, camp, picnic, or just stretch your legs at Lakeport State Park. With a mile of Lake Huron shoreline and a 284-site campground, the 565-acre park is a favorite getaway for city folk from Southeast Michigan.

With the bucolic countryside of Sanilac and Huron counties to the west, and the rocky beach and sky blue waters of Lake Huron to the east, Highway M25 passes along the edges of two worlds: the land of farming and the realm of tourism. Agriculture flourishes here in the flat, rich landscape, where fields of beans, grain, and sugar beets stretch to the horizon. On the water side, beaches, marinas, public parks, and campgrounds lure tourists and fishermen to Huron's clear, cool water. The towns along the coast meld the practicality and quaintness of farming communities with the accommodations and laid-back attitude of Michigan tourist country. Each town along the coast has its own story and unique attractions.

It's hard to imagine as you pass through the pastoral landscape of Michigan's "Thumb" that this quiet country has seen the worst of fire and storm. On September 5, 1881, midday turned to dusk as the smoke from a forest fire spread over the Thumb. Behind the cover of the unnatural darkness, a wall of flame 50 to 100 feet high raced over the land. By the time the fire burned itself out, 280 people had lost their lives and 15,000 were homeless. The newly formed American Red Cross mounted a tremendous disaster relief operation to assist the victims of the fire.

Thirty-two years after fire ravaged the landscape of the Thumb, the wind, water, and snow of a Great Lakes hurricane brought more misery to southern Lake Huron. Strong storms on the Great Lakes, especially Superior, are not uncommon in November and are never taken lightly, but the sailors on the lower lakes rarely suffer through the ferocious autumn storms that lash Lake Superior. The three-day storm of 1913 was an unfortunate exception.

When two weather systems—one dragging cold air down from Canada and the second bringing warm, moist air north—collided near the Great Lakes, a hundred-year storm was unleashed. A counterclockwise storm rotation brought the winds of each front into phase, sending a north wind tearing down the length of Lake Huron at sustained speeds of 70 miles per hour. Waves 35 feet high swamped ships, and wind-driven snow buried towns as the storm raged over the Great Lakes. Lower Lake Huron suffered the most from the storm's fury as waterfront property, harbors, and beaches were torn apart. Out on Lake Huron, eight vessels and their combined crew of 199 sailors were lost, making the Big Blow of 1913 the most deadly and costly maritime storm in Michigan's history.

The tragedies and triumphs of the people of Michigan's Thumb are remembered in the museums and by the historical societies found in nearly every town along Highway M25. Old schoolhouses, Victorian homes, lighthouses, and the retired relics of life along Lake Huron are found everywhere; all are well maintained and cared for by people who are proud of their past. Even with the hectic world of urban America so close by, the Thumb has maintained a rural, slow-paced, and friendly character that is engaging and refreshing.

INDEX

SUGGESTED READING

Dufresne, Jim. *Michigan off the Beaten Path*. Chester, CT: The Globe Pequot Press, 1988.

Hunt, Mary and Don, Hunt. *Highlights of Michigan*. Albion, MI: Midwestern Guides Publications, 1994.

Kaecher, Dan. Midwest Living *Weekend Getaways*. Des Moines, IA: Meredith Corp., 1998.

Powers, Tom. *Michigan State and National Parks*. Davison, MI: Friede Publications, 1993.

Powers, Tom. *Natural Michigan*. Davison, MI: Friede Publications, 1987.

ABOUT THE AUTHOR

ROBERT W. DOMM

Robert Domm is a lifelong Michigan resident and outdoor enthusiast. He enjoys back-country camping, canoeing, kayaking, and hiking and, when stuck indoors, enjoys playing the acoustic guitar. Most of his youth was spent living in metropolitan Detroit, but he was fortunate enough to have parents who instilled in him a love of nature by taking his family camping, fishing, and hiking in Michigan and Ontario on a regular basis. He has a BS in biology from Eastern Michigan University, and currently works as a scientist for the hydrology group of Tetra Tech, MPS in Ann Arbor and Lansing, Michigan.

In 1990, Robert and his wife Donna from suburban Detroit to a rural area in south-central Michigan and then in 2000, to an even more rural setting outside the small town of Rives Junction. They live on nine acres, five of which they manage as wildlife habitat including an acre of replanted prairie, three natural ponds, and an acre or so of oak and maple forest.

Robert Domm specializes in large format, fine art landscape photographs of the Great Lakes region. His photographs have been featured in dozens of publications including Voyageur Press's *Our Michigan*, Audubon Field Guides, and National Geographic books; Sierra Club, Audubon, and Teldon calendars; and *National Wildlife*, *Outdoor Photographer*, and *Nature's Best* magazines. Throughout the year, Robert markets prints of his work at fine art shows and promotes nature photography with speaking engagements and seminars at nature centers, photography clubs, and conservation organizations throughout Michigan.